10 MINUTE GUIDE TO

MICROSOFT®
EXCHANGE™ 5.0

by Scott Warner

A Division of Macmillan Computer Publishing
201 West 103rd St., Indianapolis, Indiana 46290 USA

For my wife, Nancy.

©1997 by Que® Corporation

Library of Congress Catalog Card Number: 97-66493

International Standard Book Number: 0-7897-1310-1

99 98 97   8 7 6 5 4 3 2 1

Interpretation of the printing code: the rightmost double-digit number is the year of the book's first printing; the rightmost single-digit number is the num-ber of the book's printing. For example, a printing code of 97-1 shows that this copy of the book was printed during the first printing of the book in 1997.

Printed in the United States of America

Publisher Roland Elgey

Editorial Services Director Elizabeth Keaffaber

Managing Editor Thomas F. Hayes

Acquisitions Editor Martha O'Sullivan

Acquisitions Coordinator Michelle Newcomb

Technical Specialist Nadeem Muhammed

Product Development Specialist John Gosney

Technical Editors Bill Bruns, Ted Henson, Michael Patten

Production Editor Audra Gable

Book Designer Barbara Kordesh

Cover Designer Dan Armstrong

Production Team Laura Knox, Darlena Murray, Terri Edwards, Paul Wilson, Donna Wright

Indexer Tim Tate

WE'D LIKE TO HEAR FROM YOU!

As part of our continuing effort to produce books of the highest possible quality, Que would like to hear your comments. To stay competitive, we *really* want you, as a computer book reader and user, to let us know what you like or dislike most about this book or other Que products.

You can mail comments, ideas, or suggestions for improving future editions to the address below, or send us a fax at 317-581-4663. For the online inclined, Macmillan Computer Publishing has a forum on CompuServe (type **GO QUEBOOKS** at any prompt) through which our staff and authors are available for questions and comments. The address of our Internet site is **http://www.mcp.com/que** (World Wide Web).

In addition to exploring our forum, please feel free to contact me personally to discuss your opinions of this book: I'm **104436,2300** on CompuServe and **jgosney@que.mcp.com** on the Internet.

Although we cannot provide general technical support, we're happy to help you resolve problems you encounter related to our books, disks, or other products. If you need such assistance, please contact our Tech Support department at 800-545-5914 ext. 3833.

To order other Que or Macmillan Computer Publishing books or products, please call our Customer Service department at 800-835-3202 ext. 666.

Thanks in advance—your comments will help us to continue publishing the best books available on computer topics in today's market.

John Gosney
Product Development Specialist
Que Corporation
201 West 103rd Street
Indianapolis, Indiana 46290
USA

CONTENTS

INTRODUCTION

The *10 Minute Guide to Microsoft Exchange 5.0* is a guide to learning about the important features of this new and powerful software. Each lesson provides step-by-step instructions on a specific feature or function of Microsoft Exchange Client.

WHAT IS MICROSOFT EXCHANGE CLIENT?

Microsoft Exchange Client is the software used on networking stations in organizations that have installed Microsoft Exchange Server, a robust messaging software application that gives you more power than the Exchange software that came with your windows operating system

If you're using Microsoft Exchange Client, you're connected to a network and you use that network to send messages. Correspondence that's conducted over a network is called *e-mail*. E-mail provides an electronic method for sending letters, memos, notes, and files to other people.

The contents of this book are based on the assumption that an administrator has installed your Microsoft Exchange Client software and configured it so you can work efficiently and productively.

Some things you'll learn about in this book include:

- Sending and receiving e-mail, both internally and outside of your company
- Accessing shared information in files and folders
- Scheduling your time
- Keeping track of contacts
- Organizing to-do lists
- Delegating mail functions
- Handling messages automatically while you're out of the office

- Working at home or on the road and then synchronizing all your files

- Accessing information from an Exchange Server using a Web browser

WHAT IS THE 10 MINUTE GUIDE TO MICROSOFT EXCHANGE 5.0?

This 10 Minute Guide offers a quick way to learn about the important features of Microsoft Exchange Client. Concise lessons guide you through specific tasks, giving you hands-on practice. Each lesson should take about 10 minutes to complete.

The book assumes that you have some experience with Windows, that you know how to use a mouse, and that you understand how to use menus and toolbars. Beyond that, use your own judgment to determine what you're ready for: You can start at the beginning and go through all the lessons, or you can jump directly to a lesson that interests you.

CONVENTIONS USED IN THIS BOOK

This book uses the following conventions to help you distinguish important information:

What you type	Things that you have to type appear in bold blue type.
Things you select	Keys that you need to press and items that you need to select appear in blue type.
On-screen text	On-screen messages from Microsoft Exchange appear in bold type.

For additional help, there are three special elements throughout this book, each of which is identified with its own icon:

 Timesaver Tips are suggestions for faster completion of a task and some useful information about the task.

 Plain English elements define Microsoft Exchange Client terminology, or computer jargon.

 Panic Button icons give some insight into avoiding potential problems.

ACKNOWLEDGMENTS

I would like to thank Martha O'Sullivan, John Gosney, and Audra Gable for their work on this book. Their expertise and professionalism combine to make Que books the biggest and best computer book publisher in the world. In addition, I would like to thank John McGrady for his help in completing this book.

TRADEMARKS

All terms mentioned in this book that are known to be trademarks have been appropriately capitalized. Que cannot attest to the accuracy of this information. Use of a term in this book should not be regarded as affecting the validity of any trademark or service mark.

WELCOME TO EXCHANGE

In this lesson, you learn how Microsoft Exchange handles the interaction between the Exchange Client software installed on your computer (also known as the workstation or the Exchange Client) and the Exchange Server software installed on the network server. The server software is what controls the exchange of messages between your computer and others on the network.

UNDERSTANDING MICROSOFT EXCHANGE SERVER

Your Microsoft Exchange software is part of Microsoft Exchange Server, a network-wide system that's been installed in your company to handle messaging, scheduling, and other exchanges of information among employees, as well as between employees and the outside world.

Microsoft Exchange Server consists of two components:

- **The server.** A server is a computer that contains information valuable to one or many users. Placing information on a server makes it available to multiple users simultaneously. This information could include annual reports, graphics, spreadsheets, or anything else that can be stored electronically. In the case of an Exchange Server, the server also holds users' e-mail messages and schedules.

- **The client.** A client is a computer that connects to a server computer to access information. Client computers are also called *workstations*. Workstations use the Exchange client software to connect to an Exchange Server. Then, workstations send and receive e-mail messages and/or update and retrieve schedule information.

There are a number of elements within each of these two components, and they all work together to accomplish tasks across a network or a group of networks.

THE EXCHANGE CLIENT SOFTWARE

The client software for Microsoft Exchange Server runs on the following operating systems:

- Windows 3.1
- Windows for Workgroups 3.1
- Windows NT 3.51 Workstation
- Windows NT 4.0 Workstation
- Windows 95
- Macintosh 7.x

While the client software also runs on DOS (version 5.0 or later), only messaging functions are supported; all other features are inaccessible.

The Windows NT Workstation and Windows 95 versions of Exchange Server Client are the most commonly used. They also look and behave the same, so throughout this book, I'll discuss Exchange Server Client from that perspective. If you're using Windows 3.x or Macintosh, your Exchange software may look slightly different, but the functions will operate the same.

HOW CLIENT AND SERVER SOFTWARE WORK TOGETHER

Microsoft Exchange Server is a modular client/server system. It is modular because a number of different components are available, so each company can install and use the features it needs. It is client/server based because the performance of tasks takes place at both the client and the server.

Performing a client process may require information that is maintained on the server (such as getting a name from the company's e-mail address book). If this occurs, the client requests the information from the server. Upon receiving the request, the server sends the information to the client. The client can then use the data to complete a process, such as composing a message. Figure 1.1 illustrates the process that takes place when a client requests this type of information from the server.

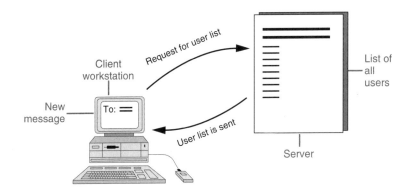

Figure 1.1   Clicking the button that displays the list of names sends a request to the server that holds that list. The server sends the list to the user's workstation, and the user selects one or more names and continues the task without any further input from the server.

Sometimes when a client sends a request to a server, the completion of the task requires a server-based process. In that case, the server proceeds with the task. For example, the client might ask the server to deliver a message to another user. Figure 1.2 shows that server process.

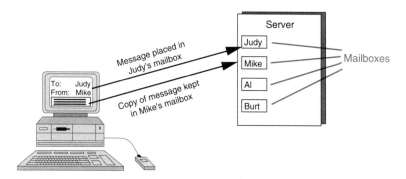

Figure 1.2   After preparing a message at the workstation, the user sends it to the recipient. This causes the message to be sent to the server, where all the mailboxes are stored. The message is placed in the recipient's mailbox, and a copy is stored in the sender's mailbox.

Understanding Objects

Object is the term used by Exchange to describe the way the elements in your Exchange software are viewed. Every element is treated as an object, including files, folders, messages, lists, and even computers. Objects are represented on your screen as icons.

Even though you see many objects in the Exchange window when you're using the software, they aren't all stored in the same place—they are just *displayed* in one place. You can't tell by looking at an object where it is stored.

Your mailbox, for example, is located on a server that is running Microsoft Exchange, and you are connected to that server. The server receives the messages you've composed and sends them to the server-based mailboxes of the recipients. When other users send mail to you, it is placed in your mailbox.

If your company has multiple locations, and therefore has installed multiple Microsoft Exchange servers, the administrators have devised a system of delivering mail among all the servers.

Your mailbox name appears on the list of users all through your company, and the mailbox names displayed on your computer include everyone in your company. When you send a message, you can't tell where the recipient is, or to which server that recipient is attached. But it doesn't matter. Microsoft Exchange Server follows a route from server to server to get and deliver your mail.

Figure 1.3 shows how all the users end up being displayed on your computer's monitor as one group, regardless of their locations or which server they're connected to.

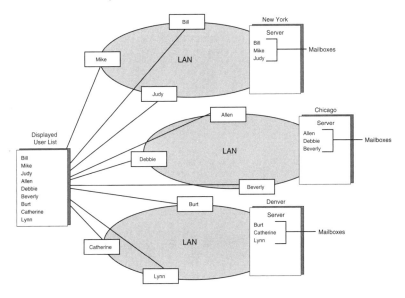

FIGURE 1.3   All the networks a company maintains have servers that are linked (usually by telephone lines). So each user sees every mailbox available in the company, no matter where the individual mailboxes are stored.

LAN LAN stands for Local Area Network. A LAN consists of computers that are grouped together. They are connected by wiring and software that allows them to communicate with each other. A company may have many separate LANs at a single location, or they may establish a single LAN at each office they maintain. Regardless of its location, each LAN can be configured so that it can communicate with other LANs.

In this lesson, you learned how the Microsoft Exchange Server and the Exchange Client software work together, and what it means to be working in a client/server environment. In the next lesson, you learn how to open and close the Microsoft Exchange Client software, and you'll also learn how to use your mailbox.

EXCHANGE BASICS

2

In this lesson, you learn how to start and end a session in Exchange, and how to navigate through your mailbox folders.

STARTING EXCHANGE

To launch the Exchange client software, use one of the following methods:

- If you are using Windows 95 or Windows NT 4.0, double-click the Inbox icon on your desktop.

- If you are using Windows NT 3.51 or Windows 3.x, open the Microsoft Exchange program group and double-click the Microsoft Exchange program icon (see Figure 2.1).

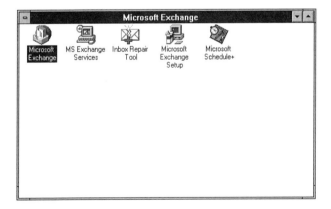

FIGURE 2.1 In Windows NT 3.51 or Windows 3.x, the Microsoft Exchange icon is inside the Microsoft Exchange program group.

THE VIEWER

The window that opens when you start Exchange is called the *Viewer*. It contains the elements found in most Windows software applications, such as a title bar, a menu bar, a toolbar, and a status bar. However, a few additional elements make the Viewer a bit different from other software windows (see Figure 2.2).

FIGURE 2.2 The Exchange Viewer is divided into panes and contains objects.

The Viewer is an object-based window, and it displays objects in a hierarchical view. The Viewer is divided into two panes:

- The pane on the left (the Folder pane) displays the folders you have access to.

- The pane on the right (the Contents pane) shows the contents of the folder that is selected in the left pane. The right pane also contains column headings to indicate the information available for the displayed contents. The column headings change according to the types of objects that are displayed.

Hierarchical View A hierarchy is a group of objects organized into classes. Each class is subordinate to the class it belongs to. This grouping can be displayed by showing the top class with each subordinate class below it. Then the subclasses of the subordinate classes can be displayed under their parents, and so on. The resulting hierarchical view shows each class and its subclasses.

THE MAILBOX

The Mailbox object displayed in the left pane represents your server-based mailbox into which messages are placed. Normally, your mailbox has four folders: Deleted Items, Inbox, Outbox, and Sent Items. However, you can add more folders (see Lesson 13 for details).

THE INBOX FOLDER

The Inbox folder receives the mail that's sent to you. When you highlight the Inbox in the Folder pane, the Contents pane displays all the messages in your Inbox (see Figure 2.3). Incidentally, the number in parentheses next to the Inbox indicates the number of unopened (unread) messages. It does not necessarily represent the total number of messages in your Inbox because you may not have disposed of previously opened messages. Notice that the status bar indicates the number of unread messages and the total number of messages in the Inbox.

THE COLUMNS IN THE CONTENTS PANE

The columns in the Contents pane break down information about the displayed objects. By default, the columns for received messages are (from left to right):

- **Importance**   This shows the priority (high, low, or normal) the sender placed on each message.

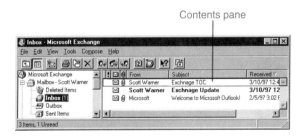

FIGURE 2.3   Click the Inbox object to see the messages that are waiting for you.

- **Item Type**   This indicates the type of message. (Message types are discussed later in this lesson.)

- **Attachment**   This contains an icon if a file or other object is attached to a message.

- **From**   This contains the name of the sender.

- **Subject**   This displays the subject of the message, which is provided by the sender.

- **Received**   This shows the date and time the message was placed in your mailbox.

- **Size**   This gives the size of the message (in kilobytes).

Configure the Columns   You can add or remove column headings, change the order in which columns appear, and change the width of the columns by choosing View, Columns and following the instructions for changing the column display.

Re-Sort the Message List   If you click a column title, the messages are sorted according to the selected column title. By default, the messages are sorted by the date they were received (the list is in descending order starting with the most recent date and time). A small arrow indicating ascending or descending order appears in the column header that is currently being used for sorting the list.

THE LIST OF MESSAGES

The Contents pane is designed to give you some information about each message through the use of the following icons:

- A plain envelope in the Item Type column represents a standard message. In addition, you may see icons representing faxes or special forms that have been designed for use in your company.

- An envelope with a padlock on it represents an encrypted message (called a "sealed" message) that requires a password to open.

- An envelope with a pen on it represents a message containing a digital signature (called a "signed" message) and requires a password to open.

- A paper clip in the Attachment column means there is an attachment to the message.

- A red exclamation point in the Importance column indicates the sender has marked the message for high priority.

- A blue down arrow in the Importance column indicates the sender has marked the message for low priority.

- Messages that are bold are new and have not been opened.

UNDERSTANDING SIGNED AND SEALED MESSAGES

"Signed" and "sealed" are Microsoft Exchange terms for special security measures that can be applied to messages:

- A signed message is one to which the sender has added an attribute that requires a recipient password. This ensures that only the recipient can open the message.

- A sealed message is one in which the contents are encrypted. A password is required to open it and read it.

These functions are part of the Advanced Security features of Microsoft Exchange Server and are not automatically available. If Advanced Security has been enabled on your Microsoft Exchange system, your system administrator will give you the information you need to apply security measures to your messages.

THE DELETED ITEMS FOLDER

Deleting a message in Exchange is a bit different from deleting files from other Windows applications, such as File Manager or Explorer. When you highlight a file and press Delete (or choose Delete from the File menu), you will not see a confirmation message such as **Are you sure?** or **Do you really want to delete this file?** Instead, the message just disappears from the list in the Contents pane.

 It's Not Really Gone! When you delete a message, it is merely moved to the Deleted Items folder. If necessary, you can rescue your deleted messages before they disappear permanently (see Lesson 11 for details). While this is similar to the Recycle Bin of Windows 95 and Windows NT 4, it is in no way associated with the Recycle Bin.

THE OUTBOX FOLDER

The Outbox is the container that holds messages you've sent until those messages are delivered to the server. The system checks the Outbox for mail and sends messages either immediately upon your command or at a specified time, depending on the choices you make. (See Lesson 7, "Composing and Sending Messages," for more information on your choices for when to send mail.) You can delete a message from the Outbox if you change your mind about sending it.

THE SENT ITEMS FOLDER

After you send a message, a copy is placed in the container called the Sent Items Folder. This is useful if you need to refer to the message after it's sent or if you need to be reminded about the original message when you receive a reply from the recipient. For example, if you receive a message in response to your own e-mail, and the text of the message you receive consists of a single word like "Yes" or "Thursday," you have to remember the question you asked that engendered that answer. Looking in the Sent Items folder saves you the embarrassment of having to ask your correspondent what the original question was in order to make sense of the answer.

QUITTING EXCHANGE

There are two methods you can use to quit Exchange. Regardless of which method you use, your Microsoft Exchange Client software closes, and you don't have access to its features. However, the method you use to quit has an effect on any other messaging applications that may be running on your computer.

Messaging Application   Software that uses the messaging features provided by the operating system is called Messaging Application Programming Interface (MAPI). MAPI provides addressing, sending, receiving, and storing functions for messages. Software programmers use these functions to add messaging features to software. For example, there are word processors that provide some levels of messaging, enabling you to send documents to other network users while you are using the word processor (without opening Microsoft Exchange Client).

To quit Exchange, use one of the following methods:

- Choose File, Exit or click the Close (X) button to quit Exchange. This closes the Microsoft Exchange Client but leaves any other messaging applications running.

- Choose File, Exit and Log Off to close Microsoft Exchange Client and all other messaging applications.

In this lesson, you learned about opening and closing Exchange, and you gained some understanding about Exchange's appearance. You also learned about the components of your mailbox. In the next lesson, you will learn how to use the Help files in Exchange.

3

LESSON

GETTING HELP

In this lesson, you learn how to use the Help feature in Exchange to get assistance as you perform tasks. You'll also learn how you can add your own notes to the information you find in the Help files.

FINDING HELP

This lesson discusses the Microsoft Exchange Server help features found in the Help Topics dialog box. To access this dialog box, choose Help, Microsoft Exchange Help Topics. The Help Topics dialog box appears, as shown in Figure 3.1. The Help Topics dialog box has three tabs available, so you can choose the way you search for help. The help features available on each of these tabs are discussed here.

FIGURE 3.1 The Help Topics dialog box.

No matter which tab you use, you end up with the same contents. Which tab you choose depends on how you want to search for help:

- Use the Contents tab to get an overview of a topic. This is useful if you want to understand how a feature works.

- Use the Index tab to find information about a broad topic by name, such as Outbox, Print, and so on.

- Use the Find tab to see all the topics that contain a specific word. When you enter the word, a list of the index topics that contain that word appears.

THE CONTENTS TAB

The Contents tab lists all the Help topics, arranged alphabetically by topic. A book icon appears to the left of each topic. To open a book, follow these steps:

1. Click the book icon next to the category you want to open, and then choose Open. When the book opens, its *chapters* (the page icons with the question marks) are listed (see Figure 3.2). When the book is open, the Open button changes to a Close button, which you can click to close the book.

2. To get to the contents, use one of these methods:

   - To display the Help page of the category you want, click the page icon and choose Display. The Help page displays a detailed explanation of the topic. (You'll learn more about the contents of the Help page later in this lesson.)

   - To print a chapter, select it and choose Print.

   - To print a book, select it and choose Print. A book can contain many chapters, so it might be faster and less wasteful to print only the specific chapters you really need.

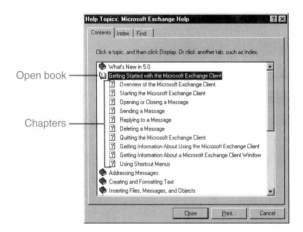

Open book

Chapters

Figure 3.2   You see a list of the chapters for each book, so you can pick the one you need.

3. Click the Contents button to return to the Contents tab.

4. Click the Close button (the X in the upper-right corner of the dialog box) to close the Help facility.

The Index Tab

When you click the Index tab in the Help Topics dialog box, the Help window changes to display the Index, which looks like a book index (see Figure 3.3). Entries are listed alphabetically, with subtopics indented below the major topics. All the major topics for which there are pages in the Help books are included.

To find a Help topic using the Index tab, follow these steps:

1. In the Type the First Few Letters of the Word You're Looking For text box, type the first letters or words of the Help topic you're looking for. As you type, the index list jumps to the first list entry that matches the characters you're typing and highlights that topic.

2. (Optional) Instead of typing the topic in the text box, scroll through the Index listings, either to get an idea of the available topics or to find a specific topic.

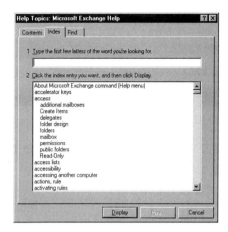

FIGURE 3.3   The Help Index tab.

3. When you get to the Index section you want, select the topic and choose Display to see the information (or click Print to print it).

THE FIND TAB

The Find tab is useful for locating Help entries when you're not sure of their Index titles. You can type a word and see all the topics that contain that word in their contents.

The first time you use the Find tab, you must create a database of words and Help files that Find uses to locate the Help topics you want. Don't worry, Exchange provides a Find Setup Wizard to help you through the process.

To create the Find database and use the Find feature, follow these steps:

1. Click the Find tab in the Help Topics dialog box. The Find Setup Wizard appears, as shown in Figure 3.4.

2. Choose the database configuration (described next) by clicking the option button next to the configuration you want. Then click Next.

FIGURE 3.4 The Find Setup Wizard.

3. After making your selection, follow the Wizard's easy instructions to complete the creation of the database for the Find tab.

When you run the Find Setup Wizard, you have three choices for configuring the database:

Minimize Database Size   Use this option to create only a database, with no additional features except for the ability to search for words.

Maximize Search Capabilities   Use this option to create a database that has added features that enable you to search for a topic and then move to other similar topics without entering a new word to search for. This database is much larger and takes longer to load when you want to use the Find tab, so don't choose this option unless you have found that working with the Minimize Database Size choice isn't providing the services you need.

Customize Search Capabilities   Use this option to make advanced decisions about how to establish the database, such as which Help files to use, whether to include topics that are not part of an Index section (some definitions are not indexed), and whether to enable the feature with which you can search for phrases instead of words and the feature that lets you mark a section and then search for

similar sections even if those similar sections don't contain
the word you typed. This database is large and is much
slower to use; if you don't need these capabilities, don't
select this choice.

 Choosing a Database Option Don't worry about making the wrong choice. You can re-establish this database with different choices by clicking the Rebuild button on the Find tab. The Find Setup Wizard then walks you through the process again.

After you create the Find database, you can use the Find feature
by following these steps:

1. In the Help Topics dialog box, click the Find tab to display it (see Figure 3.5).

FIGURE 3.5 The Find tab.

2. In the Type the Word(s) You Want to Find text box, type the words or phrase in which you are interested. As you type, matching characters appear in the next list.

3. In the Select Some Matching Words to Narrow Your
   Search box, choose one or more words that most closely
   match the topic for which you are looking.

4. Choose a topic from the Click a Topic, Then Click Display
   box. Click Display, and the Help page for that topic appears. (You'll learn more about the contents of the Help
   page next.)

5. (Optional) Click Print to print the contents of the Help
   topic so you can have a hard copy reference.

You Can Change the Way Find Works   To modify how
the Find feature searches for a word or phrase, choose
Options. The Find Options dialog box appears, and you
can change the way the Find feature functions. The
choices are self-explanatory.

UNDERSTANDING THE CONTENTS OF A HELP PAGE

When you use one of the methods described earlier in this lesson
to choose the specific Help topic you want, a Help topic page
appears. Most Help pages have more than helpful text; there are
additional features and functions with which you can get even
more help (see Figure 3.6).

The following sections describe the elements of the Help page
shown in Figure 3.6.

HELP PAGE MENU BAR

You can use the options on the menu bar to perform tasks or
access features. All the choices on all the menu items are not
described here (although you may want to do that when you have
some time to explore your system). Here are some of the most
useful commands:

Annotate You can use the Annotate command to add your own notes or comments to the displayed Help topic. Choose Edit, Annotate, and the Annotate dialog box appears. Type your notes in the Current Annotation text box, and then click Save to close the dialog box and return to the Help page. When you add an annotation to a Help page, a paper clip icon appears to the left of the first sentence of the contents. The next time you display this Help page, you can click the paper clip to see your note.

Bookmarks Bookmarks are used to mark those pages you think you might want to return to frequently. The first time you open the Bookmark menu, it contains only one choice: Define. Just click OK to create the bookmark. When you create a bookmark for a page, it is added to the Bookmark menu. To find a favorite Help page, choose Bookmark and click the bookmark of the page you want. You're taken to that Help page immediately.

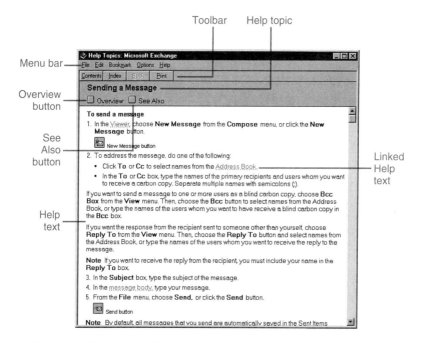

FIGURE 3.6 A typical Help page.

THE HELP TOPIC TOOLBAR

The toolbar buttons on the Help page enable you to perform the following functions:

- Contents returns you to the Contents tab of the Help system.
- Index returns you to the Index tab of the Help system.
- Back moves you back to the previous Help topic page. (The Back button is grayed out and inaccessible if you are on the first page that appeared after you selected a topic.)
- Print prints the currently displayed topic.

For some reason, there is no toolbar button for returning to the Find tab of the Help system. I find the easiest way to get there from here is to click Index and then click the Find tab.

OVERVIEW

Some topic pages have an Overview button below the topic title. You can click it at any time to see an overview of the general topic that the current page is a part of.

SEE ALSO

Click the See Also button to see other topics that include a reference to or additional information about the current topic.

LINKED HELP TEXT

You can click any text that is underlined (and appears in a different color) to see its definition. Text underlined with dashes is linked to definitions, and text underlined with a solid line is linked to other topics.

FINDING HELP IN EXCHANGE'S DIALOG BOXES

Up to now, this lesson has covered the main Help system. However, it's important to note that within the features of Microsoft Exchange Client, most of the dialog boxes and windows you use also have their own Help feature.

If a dialog box has a Help button, you can click it to see specific help about the options on that dialog box.

If any dialog box has a question mark in the upper-right corner, it means that the "What's This?" feature is active. To learn about any part of the dialog box, click the question mark, and then click any title or text in the dialog box to see its definition. Or, you can right-click any title or text in the dialog box and click the small box that says What's This? to see the definition.

In this lesson, you learned how to find specific Help topics and how to take advantage of special features available on the Help pages in Exchange. In the next lesson, you'll learn about the Global Address List.

USING THE GLOBAL ADDRESS LIST

In this lesson, you learn about e-mail addresses and how to find a user using the Global Address list.

THE PURPOSE OF THE GLOBAL ADDRESS LIST

Before you learn how to create mail messages, it's important that you know about the Global Address List and how to access and use it. The Global Address List is a directory of all users to whom you can address mail. The list is maintained by the administrators of your Exchange system and is stored on the Microsoft Exchange server. In addition to listing individuals, the Global Address List can include folders, and you can send messages or files to those folders.

DISPLAYING THE GLOBAL ADDRESS LIST

You can access the Global Address List from two places in your Microsoft Exchange Client software: the Tools menu and a message form. The two resulting displays are slightly different in appearance, and there are some differences in the way you use them.

ACCESSING THE LIST FROM THE TOOLS MENU

Choose Tools, Address Book to display the Address Book dialog box (see Figure 4.1).

FIGURE 4.1   The Address Book dialog box displays the Global Address List.

 It's Not the Global Address List Exchange clients can use more than one address book. In the Show Names from the: drop-down list, select Global Address List (if necessary) to view that list of names.

You cannot add or delete any names from the Global Address List because it is administered by Microsoft Exchange Server administrators. However, you can use the menu options and toolbar buttons to get information about any user on the list.

You can get additional information about anyone in the list by selecting the user's name and clicking the Properties toolbar button (or by double-clicking the name). The Properties dialog box displays any additional information that is available for the selected user (see Figure 4.2).

From the Properties dialog box, you can obtain the following information about any person on the Global Address List:

- **Distribution List Membership** You can find out which distribution lists this member is on by selecting the Member Of tab. (Distribution lists are covered in Lesson 6.)

- **Exact E-Mail Address**   You can check the exact e-mail address for the user by selecting the E-Mail Addresses tab. This is useful if the user is a *custom recipient*, not a user from your company. (You'll learn more about e-mail addresses later in this lesson.)

In addition, you can copy any name on the Global Address List to your own personal address list, which you'll learn about in the next lesson.

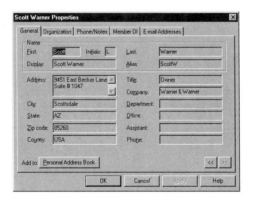

Figure 4.2   If the administrators have added any optional information to the user information, you can view it.

   Custom Recipient   A user listed in an address book who is reached through another system (who is not an employee of your company). Someone reached through the Internet, CompuServe, or a mainframe message system such as PROFS is a custom recipient.

Accessing the Global Address List from a Message Form

When you compose a message (by clicking the New Message button), you can display the Global Address List by clicking the To:, Cc:, or Bcc: button in the New Message form (see Figure 4.3). You can select one or more users as recipients of your message. Lesson 7 explains how to select a recipient when you create a new message.

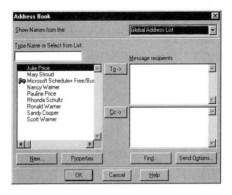

FIGURE 4.3   Select a user from the Global Address List, and then choose To: to add the user as a recipient for a new message.

UNDERSTANDING E-MAIL ADDRESSES

When you send mail, you're sending it to an address that is unique to the recipient. Likewise, you have a unique address, which a person must know in order to send you mail. Although there are many e-mail address types, Microsoft Exchange Server provides features to ensure that your administrators have a way of establishing whatever address types the users in your company may need.

The e-mail address configured for you is accessible to other users in your company. Like you, they see a list of users when they compose messages, and they can choose your name from the list when they want to send you a message.

However, the list that's displayed when users are working in Microsoft Exchange Client is not really a list of e-mail addresses; it's a list of shortcut references called *display names*. A display name refers to a user's mailbox the same way that an e-mail address does.

USING THE FIND TOOL

Most companies have a long list of e-mail addresses, and you can click the Find button to speed up the search for a particular user. When the Find dialog box appears, you enter information to help the Find tool locate the user you need (see Figure 4.4). When you're trying to find a user, the more information you fill out, the narrower and faster the search will be. Generally, a user only needs to know the recipient's complete address if he wants to send mail to someone outside of his company; when sending to someone within the company, all he needs to know is the person's alias or display name.

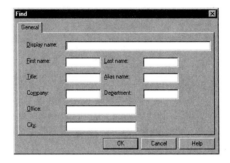

FIGURE 4.4   Each information box that you fill out helps to narrow the search and make it more efficient.

In this lesson, you learned about the Global Address List that is used to send messages to users inside your company and outside your company. In the next lesson, you'll learn how to create your own personal address list.

USING PERSONAL ADDRESS BOOKS

In this lesson, you learn how to create a personal address book, so you can keep your own list of message recipients.

CREATING A PERSONAL ADDRESS BOOK

A personal address book (PAB) is a list of addresses that you can create, customize, and use for sending messages. This is your own personal list and is not visible to any other users. You can add and delete names as necessary to keep your PAB up-to-date and useful.

Before you can begin using your PAB, you have to create it. This is a two step process. First, you add the Personal Address Book to the list of Microsoft Exchange Client services you want to use. Then you create the Personal Address Book. The following two sections walk you through those processes.

ADDING THE PAB TO EXCHANGE CLIENT SERVICES

By default, the installation process for Microsoft Exchange Client does not give you the option of having PABs. The administrators who installed your software might have added this option for you, but if they didn't, you can easily add it yourself. To see if you have a PAB option or to add the option, choose Tools, Services to display the Services dialog box (shown in Figure 5.1).

FIGURE 5.1 The Services dialog box.

If Personal Address Book is listed there, you're all set. If not, follow these steps to add the PAB to your Microsoft Exchange Client software and to customize some of its features:

1. In the Services dialog box, click Add to display the Add Service to Profile dialog box (see Figure 5.2).

FIGURE 5.2 The Add Service to Profile dialog box.

2. Select Personal Address Book.

3. Click OK, and the Personal Address Book Properties dialog box appears.

 TIP **Accessing the PAB Service** If the PAB service was already listed in your Services dialog box, you can access the PAB Properties dialog box by selecting Personal Address Book from the list on the Services tab and choosing Properties.

4. (Optional) The PAB Properties dialog box offers the following configuration options, which you can change to customize your PAB to your own tastes and habits:

   • You can use the Path box to change the name of the PAB file from Mailbox to any other name (perhaps your own name); however, make sure you keep the .PAB file extension.

   • You can change the way names are listed (and alphabetized) by choosing First Name or Last Name.

   • You can use the Notes tab to write yourself a note or to make a comment about this PAB (which is not usually necessary unless you're planning to create multiple PABs).

5. When you finish making the desired changes (or if you're perfectly happy with the default configuration to begin with), click OK to close the PAB Properties dialog box.

If you just added the PAB service, Exchange displays a message telling you that your PAB will not be available for use until you exit and log off your current Exchange session. This is because the services available for you when you start Exchange are determined by the software as it first starts up (it reads the list in the Services dialog box). When you started this Exchange session, the PAB was not listed in the Services, so you can't use it now. However, next time you start the software, it will be listed. If you want to use the PAB right away, exit, log off and start Exchange again.

ADDING LISTINGS TO YOUR PAB

To add listings to your PAB, copy them from the Global Address List. To do this, follow these steps:

1. Choose Tools, Address Book to display the Address Book dialog box.

2. If necessary, click the Show Names From drop-down arrow and select Global Address List from the drop-down list.

3. Select a name from the list that appears.

4. Click the Add to Personal Address Book toolbar button (see Figure 5.3).

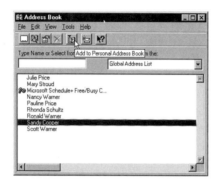

FIGURE 5.3   Select a name in the Global Address List and copy it to your Personal Address Book.

5. To look at the PAB list, click the Show Names from the drop-down arrow and select Personal Address Book. The entries in your PAB appear.

6. When you've added all the names you want to your PAB, click the Close button to exit the Address Book dialog box.

Note that if you opted to organize your PAB by last name, the entries (which are sorted by first name by default) are re-sorted and displayed by Last Name when you move them into your PAB.

TIP   **Copying Multiple Entries**   You can copy several names to your Personal Address Book at one time by selecting the first name you want to add, holding down the Ctrl key, and selecting any additional names. Then click the Add to Personal Address Book button, and all the highlighted entries are copied. If you want to copy a group of names that are listed consecutively, select the first name you want to include, hold down the Shift key, and click the last name to include.

USING THE PERSONAL ADDRESS BOOK

Because your PAB contains addresses for only the recipients you most frequently send mail to, finding the recipient you need in the PAB will be much faster than scrolling through all the names in the Global Address List.

When you need an address, you can call up an address book in either of the following ways:

- Choose Tools, Address Book.

- Open the New Message window, click the To button, click the Show Names from the drop-down arrow, and choose Personal Address Book.

In this lesson, you learned how to create a personal address book and how to add names to it. In the next lesson, you'll learn how to create distribution lists so you can send messages to groups instead of to one person at a time.

6

USING DISTRIBUTION LISTS

In this lesson, you learn how to use distribution lists to send messages to a group of recipients.

CREATING PERSONAL DISTRIBUTION LISTS

A *distribution list* is a collection of addresses that are grouped together for some logical reason. The distribution list appears as a single entry in an address book and is treated as a single recipient. When you send a message to that recipient, the distribution is automatically expanded to include every recipient on the list.

The administrators of your Microsoft Exchange Server system may create global distribution lists for everyone to use. These lists appear in the Global Address List. The Global Address List can include multiple distribution lists.

If you often send messages to the same group of people, you should create a personal distribution list (PDL). A PDL appears as one recipient in your Personal Address Book. Distribution lists are often used in the following types of situations:

- You have a group of employees that reports to you, and you frequently send messages to them.

- You are part of a team for a project, and all team members frequently exchange messages.

- You regularly send reports to certain management people.

To create a personal distribution list, follow these steps:

1. Choose Tools, Address Book (or click the Address Book toolbar button) to display the Address Book dialog box.

2. In the Address Book dialog box, open the File menu and choose New Entry (or click the New Entry toolbar button). The New Entry dialog box appears (see Figure 6.1).

Figure 6.1 Personal Distribution Lists are a type of entry that can be added to an address book.

3. From the list of entry types, choose Personal Distribution List. Then click OK. The New Personal Distribution List Properties dialog box appears, as shown in Figure 6.2.

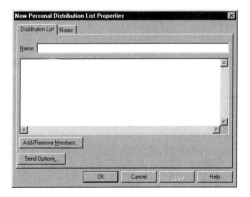

Figure 6.2 The New Personal Distribution List Properties dialog box.

4. Type a name for the distribution list in the Name text box. (It's helpful to give your list a name that reminds you of the membership, such as "Project X team.")

> **Friendly Reminder**   Click the Notes tab to add reminders or comments to yourself about this list's origin and use.

5. To add recipients to the distribution list, click Add/ Remove Members. The Edit New Personal Distribution List Members dialog box appears (see Figure 6.3). By default, the Global Address List is displayed on the left side of the dialog box.

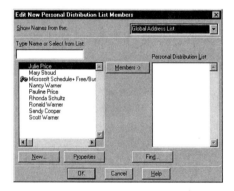

FIGURE 6.3   The Edit New Personal Distribution List Members dialog box.

6. (Optional) To display your Personal Address Book instead of the Global Address List, click the Show Names from the drop-down arrow at the top of the dialog box and select Personal Address Book.

7. In the address list on the left side of the dialog box, double-click names you want to add to your personal distribution list. The names then appear in the list on the right side of the dialog box.

8. When you finish adding to your personal distribution list, click OK.

Deleting Members from PDL   To delete a member of a personal distribution list, highlight the user's name and press the Delete key. If there is more than one user in your list, be sure to delete the semicolon after the user's name as well.

After you create your personal distribution list, it appears as a recipient in your Personal Address Book (see Figure 6.4). As you can see, the name of the distribution list appears in bold type, and an icon showing two people appears to the left of the entry.

Your new distribution list

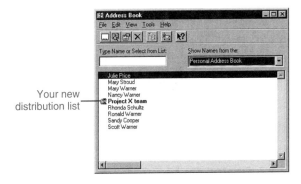

FIGURE 6.4   Distribution lists are displayed with the other entries in your Personal Address Book.

ADD LISTS TO LISTS

You can create as many personal distribution lists as you need, and you can even add existing distribution lists to new lists. If, for example, you have a personal distribution list for all the members of a project team, and you are creating a list of people to whom you send periodic summary reports about the project, you can add the project team distribution list to the new list. That way you don't have to individually enter each recipient of the project team when creating the new list. In computer jargon, including a list in a list is called *nesting*. (Microsoft Exchange Server supports nested lists.)

USING GLOBAL AND PERSONAL DISTRIBUTION LISTS

After you create a distribution list, it appears as one recipient in an address book and is treated exactly the same as an individual recipient. To send a message to all the people on the list, you just select the name of the distribution list as the recipient for a message. And you don't have to worry about the individual members of the distribution list receiving the message, because Microsoft Exchange Server will take care of it for you.

TIP   **Adding a Partial PDL**   If you want to add all but a few members of a Personal Distribution List, follow the steps you normally would to add a PDL to the recipients list. But after you select the PDL in the Address Book dialog box, click the Properties button instead of the To: button. The Personal Distribution List dialog box appears, showing several new buttons: To, Cc, and Bcc (if this field is displayed in your New Message window). Choose the recipients you would like to add and click the appropriate button. Then click OK to return to the Address Book dialog box. There you'll see that the names you selected have been added to the recipient list in the section corresponding to the button you used to add them.

If you're not sure who is included in a distribution list (especially one in the Global Address List, because you didn't create it), you can click the name of the distribution list in any dialog box or window in which the list is displayed, and then choose Properties. You might do this while you are creating a new message or examining an address book, for example.

While viewing the Properties of a personal distribution list, you can add or delete members at any time—even while you are creating a message. Note, however, that you cannot change distribution lists in the Global Address List because the system administrators control them.

In this lesson, you learned how to create and use distribution lists. In the next lesson, you'll learn how to create and send a message.

COMPOSING AND SENDING MESSAGES

In this lesson, you learn how to compose a message, identify all recipients of the message, and send the message.

COMPOSING A MESSAGE

Composing an e-mail message is similar to writing a letter and sending it to someone via the United States Postal Service. You create text, you address it with an accurate address, and sometimes you even write a note on the envelope to indicate something special about the contents inside, such as "personal" or "urgent."

The biggest difference between e-mail and USPS mail is the speed at which your message is delivered to the recipient. After you use e-mail and get used to its almost instantaneous delivery system, you'll begin to understand why computer users have adopted the jargon "snail mail" for mail sent through the USPS.

To compose a message in Microsoft Exchange Client, you carry out the following three steps, all of which are quite easy:

1. Fill out the *message header*

2. Write the message

3. Send the message

Message Header The message header is the top part of the message form, where you insert the name(s) of the recipient, the subject, and other information about the message. The header information appears in the message recipient's Inbox.

CREATING THE MESSAGE HEADER

The message header typically includes all the recipients of the message and the subject of the message. When you receive a message, you see the header information in your Inbox.

You can receive a message in any of these three ways:

- You can be the primary recipient, in which case your name is listed in the To: text box of the message.

- You can receive a carbon copy (or Cc) of the message, in which case your name(s) is listed in the Cc: text box of the message. (Names listed in the Cc: text box appear in the message window of each recipient.)

- You can receive a blind carbon copy (Bcc) of the message. In this case, your name does not appear in the message window at all. Primary and Cc recipient(s) do not know that anyone received a blind carbon copy.

Be Precise If you type the name of the recipient, make sure you spell it exactly as it appears in the address list. If a name cannot be matched to a display name, Exchange alerts you that the user does not exist and gives you the option of creating the user or choosing an alternative user with a similar name.

The subject of your message is also very important because recipients can use it to search through messages when looking for specific information. In fact, if you save the messages you send, it can also help you on those occasions when you might have a need to search for a particular subject. There also may be occasions when either you or the recipients need to gather similar messages and want to sort them so that messages with similar subjects are listed together. Therefore, try to make your wording as relevant and specific as you can. For example, entering "Peterson Supermarket Construction Project Budget" is better than "Notes about the budget for the project."

To create a header for a new message, follow these steps:

1. Click the New Message button on the toolbar (or choose Compose, New Message). The New Message dialog box appears, as shown in Figure 7.1.

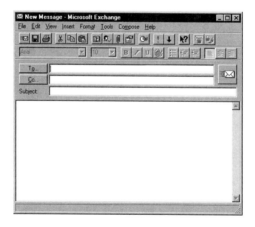

FIGURE 7.1   The New Message dialog box.

2. The insertion point is positioned in the To text box by default. Enter the names of the primary recipients, using one of the following methods:

   • Type the name(s), separating multiple recipients with semicolons (;).

- Click the To button to display the Address Book dialog box (see Figure 7.2). Choose an address list from the drop-down list at the top. Then click the name of each recipient you want to add and click the To button to add it to the recipient list.

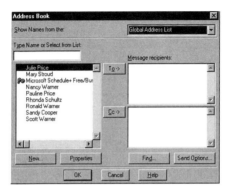

FIGURE 7.2 The Address Book dialog box.

TIP

Check Your Entries If you opt to type the names into the recipient boxes, you must be careful to enter each name exactly as it appears in the address list. To be sure you haven't made a mistake, after you enter the names you can choose Check Names from the Tools menu. Exchange matches each typed entry against the list of known mailboxes and notifies you if there's an entry that has no match (and offers a suggested alternative). When the entry is confirmed, it becomes underlined.

Last Name First? Don't worry about entering the last name first (or vice versa), even if your address list is established differently. Exchange figures it out. The To box displays the recipient the way your address book has it.

3. When you finish inserting recipients, click OK.

4. (Optional) To send a carbon copy to a recipient, type the name(s) in the Cc text box, or double-click the Cc button and enter the name(s) using the Address Book dialog box in the same way you entered primary recipients (refer to Figure 7.2).

5. (Optional) If you want to send a blind carbon copy (Bcc) of the message to a recipient, choose View, Bcc Box. A new field appears below the Cc box. Click the Bcc button to display an address list from which you can select recipients (using the same method you did to enter primary and Cc recipients).

6. In the Subject text box, enter the subject, or topic, of this message. After you enter the subject, the title bar of the New Message window changes to show the subject of your message.

ENTERING THE MESSAGE TEXT

After you fill out all the Header information, you can start typing your message. When you start entering text, you'll notice that the formatting toolbar in the message window becomes active (the buttons are no longer grayed out). This is just like using a word processor, and all those toolbar features are available to you. You will learn about them in Lesson 9.

TIP   **WordMail**   If you have Microsoft Word, you can use it as your message editor. The To, Cc, and Subject functions work the same, but the message text can be formatted using all of the features available to Word. To make Word your e-mail editor, choose WordMail Options from the Compose menu of the Exchange Client. In the WordMail Options dialog box, make sure the Enable Word As E-Mail Editor check box is checked.

ASSIGNING IMPORTANCE

You can indicate the priority of a message before you send it. You might want to change the priority of a message for reasons such as these:

- Recipients who get a lot of e-mail generally read *high* priority messages first.

- You may want to indicate to a busy recipient that this particular message is of minimal or low importance and, therefore, does not have to be read immediately.

- When your Microsoft Exchange Server system is very busy, it can be configured to move high-priority messages through the system first.

There are three priority choices: high, normal, and low. Normal is the default and requires no special action. High priority messages are marked with a red exclamation point in the recipient's Inbox. Low priority messages are marked with a blue downward-pointing arrow. Normal priority messages have no special markings.

If you want to indicate high or low priority for a message, follow these steps:

1. In the New Message window, open the View menu and select Toolbar to insert a message window toolbar above the formatting toolbar.

2. Click the exclamation point button to assign a high priority to the message, or click the downward-pointing arrow button to assign a low priority.

SENDING THE MESSAGE

When you complete your message, it's time to send it. You can send it immediately, or you can specify that you want to send it at a later time.

- To send the message right away, click the Send button (or choose File, Send or press Ctrl+Enter).

- If you want to delay sending the message, choose File, Send Options to display the Send Options dialog box (see Figure 7.3). Click the In option, enter a number, and choose whether you want the message to be sent in that number of minutes, hours, days, or weeks.

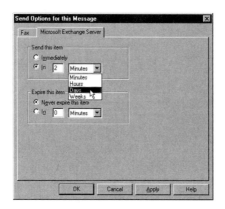

FIGURE 7.3   You can specify the amount of time that elapses before the message is sent.

If you delay sending the message, a copy is placed in the Outbox folder of your mailbox. If you change your mind about sending it, you can delete it from the Outbox. If you want to change the Send options, you can select the message in the Outbox folder and choose File, Properties. Then, from the Properties dialog box, you can change the send options. After the message is sent, a copy is placed in the Sent Items folder of your mailbox.

In this lesson, you learned how to compose and send a message. In the next lesson, you'll learn how to attach items such as files to your messages.

ATTACHING ITEMS TO MESSAGES

8

*In this lesson, you learn how to attach files or other
items to a message. You also learn how to access and use
attachments that are in messages you receive.*

WHAT IS AN ATTACHMENT?

An attachment is a file or an object that is attached to a message.
You can place attachments in messages you send, and you can
receive messages with attachments.

The usefulness of attachments is unlimited, but the most common reason for attaching a file to a message is to send some information without having to type it into the original message. For
example, if you want to send information you received (or wrote)
in a word processing document to another member of your organization, you can compose a message that explains that you have
this information (and perhaps offers some comments on it), and
then you can attach the specified document to the message so the
recipient can read the information for herself.

ATTACHING FILES TO MESSAGES

You can attach an existing file to a message with just a few key-
strokes or mouse clicks. There are a couple of things to be aware
of, however, before you try this.

- If the file is a text file (one that does not have specific
  software codes and can be opened and viewed with any
  text editor), you can attach the file to any message for
  any recipient.

- If the file was prepared by a specific software application, the recipient must have access to that software to open and view the file.

- If you are sending an attachment to someone with a slow-speed connection to the network, a large attachment could take a long time to download. To be safe, you should compress large files before sending them.

Taking those guidelines into consideration, if you want to send a message with an attachment, first prepare the message as usual (see Lesson 7 for information on composing a message). Then follow these steps:

1. Put your insertion point at the place in the message where you want to insert the icon to indicate the attached file.

2. Choose File, Insert. The Insert File dialog box appears, as shown in Figure 8.1.

FIGURE 8.1 Browse through your folders to find the document file you want to attach to the message.

3. In the File Name text box, enter the name of the file you want to insert. (If you don't know the name of the file, you can use the Look In box to search for the file. When

you find it, select it, and its name appears in the File Name text box.)

4. In the Insert As section at the bottom of the dialog box, select An Attachment.

5. Click OK, and an icon with the document name appears in the text area where you placed the insertion point. As in other Windows applications, the icon that represents a file is the icon for the application associated with that file (see Figure 8.2).

Attachments for Non-Exchange Users   If you send an attachment to users who are not using Exchange, they may not see the icon that is associated with the attachment. To avoid any confusion, you could reference the attachment in your message text and identify the program used to create it.

This attachment was created in Microsoft Word.

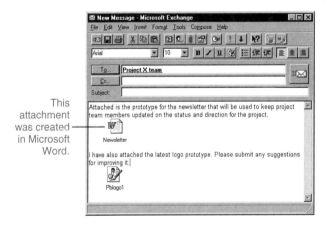

FIGURE 8.2   The icon for the attachment appears in your message.

TIP

Plain Text Attachment   If the attachment you want to send is a plain text file, you have two choices for getting the contents to the recipient:

• You can insert it as an attached file icon into your message, as described earlier.

• You can insert the text of the file into the message by selecting Text Only in the Insert File dialog box.

RECEIVING AN ATTACHMENT

When a message with an attachment arrives in your mailbox, a paper clip icon appears in the Attachment column of your Inbox (see Figure 8.3).

Represents an attachment

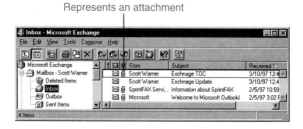

FIGURE 8.3   It's easy to tell when there's a message with an attachment in your mailbox.

To open the message, select it and choose File, Open (or double-click the message header). The message appears, along with the icons for attachments (refer to Figure 8.2).

Security   You could receive many files through e-mail. Be cautious, however, when you receive e-mail with attachments from an unknown source. File attachments may contain viruses that could damage or adversely affect your computer.

To open an attachment, double-click its icon. The associated software starts, and the attachment file opens. At that point, you can use the features of that program to edit, print, or otherwise manipulate the file.

 Editing an Attachment   If you receive a message with an attachment that is a shortcut to the original file, a pointer to the original file (not a copy of it) was sent to you. Opening this shortcut actually opens the original file. Editing the original file changes it for all users on the network, so be careful to make only serious changes that you have authority to make.

In this lesson, you learned about attachments: how to add them to messages you send and how to access those you receive with messages. In the next lesson, you'll learn more about editing and formatting the text of messages.

EDITING, SPELL CHECKING, AND FORMATTING TEXT

In this lesson, you learn how to edit and format the text you enter in your Exchange messages. You also learn how to use the spelling tool.

USING THE EDIT FUNCTIONS

Microsoft Exchange Client provides the standard editing functions you find in most word processors, a spell-checker, and a robust set of features for formatting text. Editing makes working with text easier and faster; spell checking saves embarrassment; and formatting lets you add emphasis, style, and desktop publishing standards to your message.

If you regularly use a Windows-based word processor, you can skip this section because the Edit menu functions in the Exchange message window are the same as those in your word processor. However, in case word processing is not part of your daily work, here is an overview of the functions available in the Edit menu:

- **Undo** undoes the last action you performed. For example, if you accidentally delete some text, choose Undo to bring it back. Ctrl+Z is a shortcut for Undo.

- **Cut** removes selected (highlighted) text from your message and places it on the Clipboard. Ctrl+X is a shortcut for Cut.

- **Copy** makes a copy of selected text (the text remains in the message) and places it on the Clipboard. Ctrl+C is a shortcut for Copy.

- **Paste** places a copy of the data that's on the Clipboard into your message, at the insertion point. (The data remains on the Clipboard for other Paste procedures until you place something else on the Clipboard.) Ctrl+V is a shortcut for Paste.

- **Find** opens a dialog box in which you can enter specific text you want to look for in your message. For long messages, this is faster than scrolling through the message and looking for the word or phrase you need. Ctrl+Shift+F is a shortcut for Find.

- **Replace** opens a dialog box in which you can enter specific text you want to find and replace with other particular text. For example, you might need to Find all instances of "Smith" and replace them with "Smythe." Ctrl+H is a shortcut for Replace.

 Clipboard   An area of memory in which Windows holds specified data until you replace it with new data or you exit Windows. You place data on the Clipboard using either the Cut or Copy command from the Edit menu. You can place Clipboard data in any document prepared in a Windows software application by selecting Edit, Paste.

USING THE SPELLING TOOL

Exchange provides a spelling tool that you can use to check all the words in your message. The spelling tool looks for any word that is not in its internal dictionary; when it finds one, it displays the word in the Spelling dialog box.

The spelling tool works in two different ways:

- If you select (highlight) text, it checks that text for spelling errors. This is useful if you've just typed a word, and it doesn't look right. After checking the spelling of the selected text, the spelling tool asks if you want it to check the entire document.

- If you have not selected text, the spelling tool begins checking at the location of your insertion point and moves down through the message. It then returns to the top of the message and works downward until it reaches the original starting point.

In addition to checking the message text, the spelling tool checks the text in the Subject box of the message header. Attachments are not checked for spelling.

To spell-check your messages, follow these steps:

1. Open the message that you want to spell-check.

2. Choose Tools, Spelling. If the spelling tool finds an error, it displays the Spelling dialog box shown in Figure 9.1.

FIGURE 9.1 The Spelling dialog box.

3. When the spelling tool displays a word that's thought to be misspelled, you have a number of choices:

   - Choose Ignore if you want to skip this specific occurrence of the word.

   - Choose Ignore All if you want to skip this word every time it appears in the text.

   - Choose Add to add the word to the spelling dictionary so the spelling tool will recognize it the next time you use it.

   - Choose Suggest to have the spelling tool display some words in the Suggestions list that come close to your misspelled word.

- Choose Change if the suggested word in the Change To box is the correct spelling. (You can also double-click a word in the suggested word list to change the misspelled word to the correct one.)

- Choose Change All if you want to replace all occurrences of the misspelled word throughout the document with the word in the Change To box.

No Misspelled Words?   The spelling tool displays the Spelling dialog box only if it finds a word that is not in its internal dictionary. Those words may be misspelled or they may just be proper names or technical jargon that are missing from the dictionary. If all the words in your text are in the dictionary, the dialog box never appears, and you receive an informational message telling you that the spelling check is complete.

4. The spelling tool stops at each misspelled word in your message. For each misspelled word, select one of the options outlined in step 3.

5. When the spelling tool has checked all the text, an informational message tells you that the spelling check is complete. Click OK to close the spelling tool.

Double Words   The spelling tool also checks for double words, such as "the the." When double words are displayed in the Spelling dialog box, a Delete button replaces the Change button, and you can delete one of the words.

SETTING SPELLING OPTIONS

You can configure the way the spelling tool works by configuring the Spelling options. There are three ways to reach the Options dialog box:

- Click the Options button on the Spelling dialog box while it is displaying an unrecognized word.

- Choose Tools, Options in the Message window, and then choose the Spelling tab.

- Choose Tools, Options in the Exchange window, and then choose the Spelling tab.

No matter which of these methods you use, the spelling Options dialog box appears (see Figure 9.2).

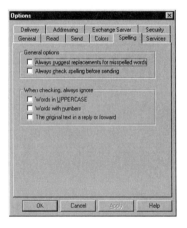

FIGURE 9.2   You can establish spelling options to suit your own convenience.

  Always Suggest   It's probably a good idea to select Always Suggest, because it saves you the trouble of clicking the Suggest button when you are facing a misspelled word.

Most of the available options should be chosen within the parameters of the type of message you usually send. For example, if you use a lot of acronyms, it's probably wise to configure the spelling tool to ignore "Words in UPPERCASE."

FORMATTING TEXT

You can change the characteristics of your text or the way specific lines are displayed in your message by using the formatting tools available on the formatting toolbar of the message window (see Figure 9.3).

FIGURE 9.3   Use the features on the formatting toolbar to enhance your messages.

The features available in the formatting toolbar are easy to understand; they are described in Table 9.1.

TABLE 9.1   FORMATTING BUTTONS

BUTTON	NAME	DESCRIPTION
Arial	Font	Displays a list of available fonts, from which you can select the one you want to use
10	Font size	Displays a list of available font sizes, from which you can select the one you want to use
B	Bold	Turns bold on and off
I	Italic	Turns italic on and off
U	Underline	Turns underline on and off

continues

TABLE 9.1 CONTINUED

BUTTON	NAME	DESCRIPTION
	Color text	Displays a list of colors you can choose from to change the color of the displayed text (and the printed text if you have a color printer)
	Bullets	Places a bullet at the beginning of each paragraph
	Decrease Indent	Decreases the indentation of a paragraph by one tab stop
	Increase Indent	Increases the indentation of a paragraph by one tab stop
	Align Left	Lines text up on the left, creating a jagged right edge
	Center	Centers each line of text between the margins
	Align Right	Lines text up on the right, creating a jagged left edge

You can add formatting as you type, or after you finish entering text. Here's how:

- If you want to add formatting as you go, select the appropriate formatting button, and then begin entering text. The buttons are *toggles*, which means that when you want to end a particular formatting style, you just click the button again to turn it off.

- If you want to format existing text, select (highlight) the text, and then click the appropriate formatting button.

Complex Formatting You can choose multiple formatting options, such as Bold and Italic, Underline and Center, or any other combination.

When to Avoid Formatting The formatting features supplied with Exchange Client are called Rich Text Formatting (RTF). A recipient must have an e-mail client that supports RTF to be able to view formatting. If you are unsure of a recipient's e-mail capabilities, consult your administrator or, to be safe, don't use formatting.

In this lesson, you learned about Microsoft Exchange Client's editing, formatting, and spell checking tools. In the next lesson, you'll learn about the options you have when receiving messages.

10

RECEIVING MESSAGES

*In this lesson, you learn how to open
and work with messages you've
received from others. You'll learn
to reply to the sender, forward to another recipient, and print copies
of messages.*

OPENING MESSAGES

Mail you receive is stored in the Inbox of your mailbox. You can
see the list of messages in the Contents pane by selecting the
Inbox object in the Folder pane (see Lesson 2 for a discussion
about the mailbox display).

When you see the list of messages in the Contents pane, the
header information helps you decide which messages to read
immediately and which messages to leave for later (if necessary).
You can use the priority icons and the subject matter to decide,
or you can just pick messages sent by people you like to hear
from.

Scroll through the list to find a message you want to open.
Double-click it, and the message opens in a message window
(see Figure 10.1).

The buttons on the message window toolbar provide quick access
to many of the options you might need for working with received
messages. Table 10.1 lists the toolbar buttons and their functions.

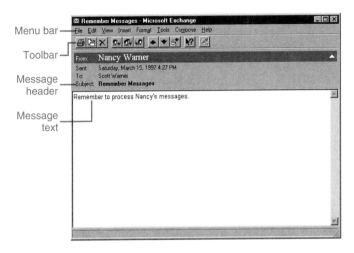

Menu bar

Toolbar

Message header

Message text

FIGURE 10.1   The text of the message appears, and the message window provides tools for working with the message.

TABLE 10.1   **TOOLBAR BUTTONS FOR WORKING WITH RECEIVED MESSAGES**

BUTTON	NAME	FUNCTION
	Print	Prints the message
	Move	Moves the message to a folder you choose
	Delete	Deletes the message
	Reply to Sender	Opens a new message window with the sender's name in the To box
	Reply to All	Opens a new message window with all recipients of the current message indicated as recipients of the new message

continues

TABLE 10.1 CONTINUED

BUTTON	NAME	FUNCTION
	Forward	Opens a new message window from which you can send this message to another recipient
	Previous	Opens the message listed immediately above the current message in the Contents pane
	Next	Opens the message listed immediately below the current message in the Contents pane
	Next Unread	Opens the next message in the Contents pane that is marked as unread
	Help	Displays information about specific elements in the received message window
	Read Digital Signature	Displays information about the password-protected signature of the sender (if advanced security is enabled)

REPLYING TO MESSAGES

You'll frequently want to reply to messages you've read. The sender may have asked a question that requires an answer from you, or you may want to make a comment about the message, or you may just want to acknowledge that you received the message.

To compose a reply to the person who sent you a message, follow these steps:

1. Open the message to which you want to reply.

2. Click the Reply to Sender button, and a new message
   window appears, already set up for your reply to the
   message you received (see Figure 10.2).

Marks the message as a reply

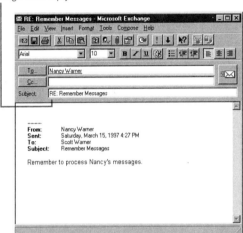

FIGURE 10.2   The message window for composing a reply.

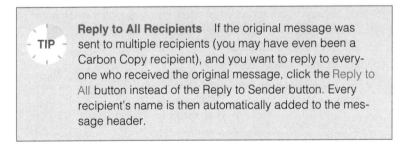

Reply to All Recipients   If the original message was
sent to multiple recipients (you may have even been a
Carbon Copy recipient), and you want to reply to everyone who received the original message, click the Reply to
All button instead of the Reply to Sender button. Every
recipient's name is then automatically added to the message header.

3. Start typing at the insertion point, which is above the
   original message (the original message is indented and a
   line appears above it to separate it from your reply). Here
   are some additional options from which you can choose:

   • If you prefer, you can move the insertion point
     below the original message to have your reply
     follow it.

- If you don't think the new recipient will need the original message in order to understand your reply, you can delete the original message.

- You can insert additional recipients in the To and Cc boxes if you want to send this reply message to others.

- You can change the text in the Subject box to reflect the contents of your reply more accurately.

- You can use all of the formatting features in your reply message.

4. When you finish composing your reply, click the Send button.

INCLUDING THE ORIGINAL MESSAGE IN YOUR REPLY

By default, the original message text is included in the reply. It is indented to make it stand out. If you want to, you can actually enter comments or notes within the original message's text.

However, if you find that most of the time you don't need to keep the original message text in your reply and you constantly have to go to the trouble of deleting it, you can change the default setup so that the original text is not automatically placed in the message section of your reply. To do so, follow these steps:

1. Choose Tools, Options to display the Options dialog box.

2. Click the Read tab to see the options shown in Figure 10.3.

3. In the second section of the box, set the following options according to your preferences:

> Deselect Include the Original Text When Replying (click to remove the check mark from the check box).

> Deselect Indent the Original Text When Replying to change the original message's position in your reply so that it starts at the left margin (if you are opting to keep the original text).

Deselect Close the Original Item if you want to keep the
original message window open while you are composing
your reply.

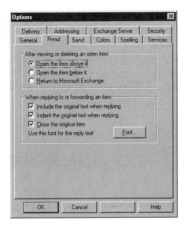

FIGURE 10.3   You can alter the default settings for replying to a
message.

4. Click the Font button to see a list of available fonts, and
   choose a new default font for all your reply messages.

5. When you finish making your changes, click OK to return
   to the Reply Message window (or click Cancel to undo
   your changes).

Keep the Original Message Open   If you choose not to
have the original text placed in your reply, you might find
it helpful to keep the original item open. That way, if you
want to check the text in the original message, it will be
available; you can just drag your reply window to the side
to see the original message behind it.

FORWARDING MESSAGES

Sometimes you receive information in a message that you think might be of interest to someone else (someone who was not sent a copy of the message). If so, you can *forward* the message, which means that you send the original message to a new recipient. You can even add your own text to the original contents if you want. To forward a message you've received, follow these steps:

1. With the message open, click the Forward button to open a new message window (see Figure 10.4).

Shows that the message is being forwarded

FIGURE 10.4   The Subject box indicates that the message is being forwarded.

2. Enter a recipient (or multiple recipients) in the To box. You can also send carbon copies to as many recipients as you want to.

3. Move your pointer into the text area to add your own comments.

4. Click Send to send the message.

Attachments Are Forwarded, Too   When you forward a message that has an attachment, the attachment is copied and sent with the forwarded message.

PRINTING MESSAGES

There might be times when you need a printed copy of a message, either to study it more carefully or to file it. You can print any message, whether you have opened it or not:

- If the message is open, click the Print button on the message window's toolbar.

- If the message is not open, select its header in the Contents pane and click the Print button on the Exchange Client window's toolbar.

Either way, the message is sent to the printer immediately. The Print dialog box does not appear, so you cannot change the printer or any other print setup configuration.

If you have to change printers or make any other adjustments to the printing process (if you want to print multiple copies, for example), you must choose File, Print or press Ctrl+P to display the Print dialog box.

Printing Attachments   By default, attachments don't print when you print a message; only the message text is sent to the printer. If you want to print the attachment, you must open the Print dialog box and select the Print Attachments option. Remember that to do this, you must have an application capable of opening and printing the file.

In this lesson, you learned how to open the messages you receive and perform several operations on them: replying, forwarding, and printing. In the next lesson, you'll learn some of the ways you can manage the storage and handling of messages.

11

MANAGING MESSAGES

In this lesson, you learn how to manage the messages you've received. You learn how to create folders to store messages, how to delete messages, and how to rescue deleted messages.

STORING MESSAGES

If you open and read a message and then close it, the message stays in the Inbox. However, you know it's been read because its header is no longer displayed in bold type. Some of those old messages can be deleted, but you'll want to save some for future reference. Fortunately, Exchange offers a number of options for storing messages.

If you delete the message, it's sent to the Deleted Items folder in your mailbox. The options for manipulating the Deleted Items folder are discussed later in this lesson.

If you want to store messages you've already read, you can create a filing system for them by creating folders and sorting the messages using whatever system suits your needs. There are two types of folders you can create to hold the messages you want to save:

- **Mailbox folders:** Folders you create that have names to match your storage scheme. These folders are part of your mailbox and are displayed in the Contents pane (along with the four folders already attached to your mailbox) when you select your Mailbox item in the Folder pane. Mailbox folders are stored on the server because they are part of your mailbox.

- **Personal folders:** Additional folders you can create for yourself. They appear in the Folder pane of your

Microsoft Exchange Client window and can be stored on your local hard drive. See Lesson 13 for information on creating and using personal folders.

CREATING AND USING MAILBOX FOLDERS

You can create folders to hold specific types of messages and keep those folders in your mailbox. For example, you may want to keep messages about a specific project all together in one folder. Or, you may use one folder for all the information you receive regarding your employee benefits and employee records, as well as other administrative messages about your organization.

While mailbox folders make it easy to find old messages, there is one thing you have to be careful about: the amount of room these folders can take up on the server. In some organizations, the administrators limit the space reserved for your mailbox in order to conserve disk space on the server. If this is true in your case, you'll want to use mailbox folders judiciously and create personal folders on your local hard drive for the messages you want to save.

 TIP   **Holding Folders**   One of the best ways to use mailbox folders is as a temporary holding bin until you can decide where to store a message permanently. This also is a good place to store any message that needs a reply from you (but not an instant reply, which you would have done while the message was open).

To create a new folder for your mailbox, follow these steps:

1. In the Folder pane, select your Mailbox item. The Contents pane lists the four default mailbox folders (Deleted Items, Inbox, Outbox, and Sent Items).

2. Choose File, New Folder to display the New Folder dialog box (see Figure 11.1).

Figure 11.1   The New Folder dialog box creates a folder that will be stored at the location of the selected item in the Folder pane.

3. Enter a name for the folder and click OK. The new folder appears in the Contents pane when your mailbox is selected (see Figure 11.2).

Figure 11.2   The new folder is displayed with the other mailbox folders (in alphabetical order).

Using Mailbox Folders

After you create a mailbox folder, it's easy to place messages in it. You can either move or copy a message into a mailbox folder, and you can perform either of those actions on both open and closed messages.

Working with Closed Messages

The easiest way to put a message into a mailbox folder is to work with a closed message, because you can simply drag the message from the list in the Contents pane into the folder. To accomplish this, follow these easy steps:

1. Make sure the mailbox folders are displayed in the Folder pane (click the plus sign next to the Mailbox object).

2. Select the Inbox folder in the Folder pane to display all messages you've received in the Contents pane, as shown in Figure 11.3.

Click the Inbox folder... ...to display mail messages.

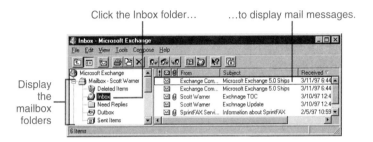

Display the mailbox folders

FIGURE 11.3 If the messages and the folders are both displayed, it's easy to drag messages to the folder of your choice.

3. To **move** a message to a mailbox folder, drag it to the folder's icon.

To **copy** a message to a mailbox folder, hold down Ctrl and drag it to the folder's icon.

TIP

Working with Multiple Messages To move or copy multiple messages, select them (hold down the Ctrl key and select each one, or hold down the Shift key and select a range). Then drag any one of the selected messages to the target folder. The others are copied or moved, too.

WORKING WITH OPEN MESSAGES

To place a message (or a copy of a message) in a mailbox folder when the message is open, follow these steps:

1. Choose File, Move or File, Copy. The Move dialog box or the Copy dialog box appears (they are the same).

2. Click the + (plus sign) next to the Mailbox object to display the mailbox folders (see Figure 11.4).

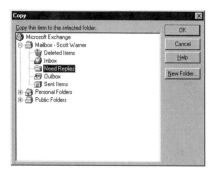

Figure 11.4   The Move and Copy dialog boxes show the objects in your Folder pane.

3. Click the folder into which you want to move or copy the open message, and then click OK.

Deleting Messages

Just as you can move or copy any message, you can also delete a message—whether it is open or closed. Deleted messages are moved to the Deleted Items folder in your mailbox. You can delete a message using either of the following methods:

- Delete an open message by clicking the Delete button on the toolbar.

- Delete a closed message by selecting it and pressing Delete (or dragging it to the Deleted Items folder in the Folder pane).

TIP   **Deleting Multiple Messages**   You can select multiple messages from the list in the Contents pane by holding down Ctrl and clicking each message you want to delete. Then press Delete to delete all the selected messages.

RETRIEVING DELETED MESSAGES

If you accidentally delete a message you need, you can retrieve it from the Deleted Items folder with these steps:

1. Select the Deleted Items folder in the Folder pane. A list of its contents appears in the Contents pane.

2. In the Contents pane, select the message you want to retrieve.

3. Choose File, Move, and the Move dialog box appears.

4. Choose the folder in which you want to place the retrieved message (usually the Inbox).

UNDERSTANDING AUTOMATIC DELETION

By default, Exchange moves messages you delete into the Deleted Items folder and keeps them there for as long as you are working in the Exchange software. When you exit Exchange, however, the messages in the Deleted Items folder are removed permanently and cannot be recovered.

 Clearing the Deleted Items Folder   When Exchange removes a message from the Deleted Items folder, it is permanently erased. It is not sent to the Recycle Bin, and it cannot be recovered.

You can change this configuration so that messages remain in the Deleted Items folder until you specifically remove them. To change this configuration, follow these steps:

1. Choose Tools, Options to access the Options dialog box. Click the General tab (if necessary) to see the options shown in Figure 11.5.

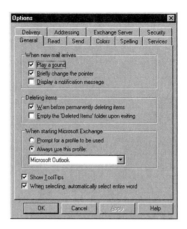

Figure 11.5   You can change your configuration to have Exchange hold deleted messages until you remove them yourself.

2. Deselect the Empty the 'Deleted Items' Folder Upon Exiting option (click to remove the check mark from the box).

3. Click OK.

Permanently Deleting Messages

If you choose to keep deleted messages after you exit Microsoft Exchange Client (i.e., until you remove them manually), your Deleted Items folder may eventually come to take up quite a bit of disk space. You should examine and empty your Deleted Items folder on a regular basis, perhaps weekly.

- To permanently delete *individual* messages, select the Deleted Items folder in the Folder pane, select the messages you can safely get rid of from the Contents pane, and then press Delete.

- To permanently delete *all* the messages in the Deleted Items folder, right-click the Deleted Items object and choose Empty Folder from the shortcut menu that appears.

Windows 3.x Users   If you're using Windows 3.x, you don't have right mouse button functions. Therefore, to remove all messages from the Deleted Items folder, you have to select the messages (Ctrl+A selects all messages) and press Delete.

In this lesson, you learned how to manage your messages and how to control the way in which Microsoft Exchange Client deletes messages. In the next lesson, you'll learn about faxing with Exchange.

LESSON 12

WORKING WITH FAXES— FOR WINDOWS 95 CLIENTS

In this lesson, you learn how to use the Windows 95 Microsoft Exchange Client to create a fax and send it. You also learn about some of the options available for sending and receiving faxes.

When Microsoft Exchange Client is installed on your workstation, you can use it for faxing instead of turning to the fax program that is part of the accessories package that came with your operating system. If you don't have a modem or network access to a shared modem, you probably don't have fax services installed in your Exchange system. Either ask your administrator about gaining fax services, or skip this lesson.

COMPOSING A FAX IN EXCHANGE

To create a fax, follow these steps:

1. Choose Compose, New Fax to start the Compose New Fax Wizard (see Figure 12.1).

2. Assuming you fax from your office computer, your location information is pre-set. Click Next in the first Fax Wizard dialog box to move on.

TIP   **Locations**   You can configure multiple location settings if you use fax services from various locations. For example, if you travel, you might have a location setting that dials special numbers to get an outside line (as you would from a hotel). If you only fax from your office and the settings never change, select I'm Not Using a Portable Computer.

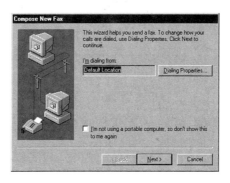

FIGURE 12.1   The Fax Wizard walks you through the process of sending a fax.

3. In the next wizard dialog box (shown in Figure 12.2), enter the name of the recipient in the To box and enter the phone number. (If the recipient is in your Address Book, click the Address Book button, choose an address list, and then choose a recipient. If the recipient is not in the Address Book, you can click New to add this recipient to the Address Book.) Click Next when you finish.

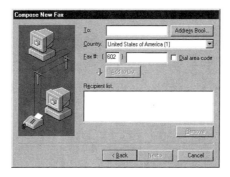

FIGURE 12.2   You enter the recipient and phone number in the Fax Wizard.

4. The next wizard dialog box asks if you want to use a cover page and gives you the opportunity to change the default options for sending faxes. These options permit you to send the fax at a later time and to include security (encryption) options. Click Options to configure these items, and then click OK to return to the wizard. When you finish this page of the Fax Wizard, click Next.

5. Fill in the Subject text box, and then enter the text of the fax in the Note section. (If you are using a cover page, there will be an option button that allows you to begin the text on the cover page instead of starting a new page.) Click Next.

6. If you want to attach a file to your fax, choose Add File in this wizard dialog box. Enter the file name in the Files to Send box. Then click Next.

Attaching Files   You can only attach files to your fax if the fax recipient uses a computer to receive faxes and has software that can open the attached documents.

7. The final wizard dialog box informs you that you have completed all the steps for composing and sending a fax. Click Finish. Your fax is either sent immediately or stored for later transmission (depending on the options you set in step 4).

Sending Faxes

Whether you send your fax immediately after composing it or at a later time, the process of sending a fax is the same. All the steps are performed automatically, and the Microsoft Fax Status dialog box reports each step of the process (preparing the fax format, dialing the number, and sending the pages). After the fax is sent, it's listed in the Sent Items folder in your mailbox.

SETTING OPTIONS FOR SENDING FAXES

You can configure the default options for sending fax transmissions so you can take advantage of lower phone rates, or you can set a specific time for sending all your faxes. (This is helpful if you're sharing a modem.)

To configure your fax sending options, follow these steps:

1. Open the Tools menu and point to Microsoft Fax Tools. A submenu appears.

2. From the submenu, choose Options to access the Microsoft Fax Properties dialog box. By default, the Message tab is displayed (see Figure 12.3).

FIGURE 12.3   Choose a default method for sending faxes; you can change the default for any individual fax.

3. Choose from the following options for sending faxes:

   • Choose As Soon As Possible if you customarily send a fax as soon as you finish preparing it.

   • If you usually send faxes over long-distance lines, choose Discount Rates and click Set. The Set Discount Rates dialog box (shown in Figure 12.4) appears. In the Start and End text boxes, enter the times for your long-distance carrier's discount period. Then click OK to return to the Microsoft Fax Properties dialog box. Exchange will attempt to send the fax in the time period you specify.

- To set a specific time for sending faxes, choose Specific Time and enter the time. Exchange will attempt to send the fax at the time you specify.

- You also can establish other configuration options on this tab, including message formats, default cover pages, and whether you can change the subject line for received faxes.

4. When you finish, click OK to return to the Exchange mailbox.

Figure 12.4   You can specify the hours during which long-distance rates are low to save money on long-distance faxes.

Receiving Faxes

Depending on your configuration options (usually established when faM services were installed), there are several ways in which your modem can respond when someone sends you a fax:

- The modem automatically answers an incoming call.

- The modem never answers a call unless you force it to.

- A dialog box appears, asking if you want the modem to answer.

By default, Exchange does not answer calls. If you have a modem attached to your computer, you'll probably want to change that option so you can receive faxes. (If faxes sent to you are received by a network modem, they're placed in your Inbox just as your e-mail is.)

TELLING THE MODEM WHETHER TO ANSWER

To set the configuration for the modem's _— avior, follow these steps:

1. Open the Tools menu, point to Microsoft Fax Tools, and select Options from the submenu.

2. Click the Modem tab.

3. Select your fax modem, and then choose Properties to display the Fax Modem Properties dialog box (see Figure 12.5).

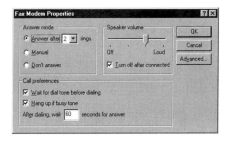

FIGURE 12.5   Reconfigure Answer Mode to have your modem answer the phone for incoming faxes.

4. Choose one of the following answer modes:

   • Select Answer After and specify the number of rings to have the modem answer the phone at that point. This is useful if you share the modem with your voice line (and generally manage to say "hello" before the number of rings you specify for modem answering).

- Choose Manual to tell the modem when to answer the phone. This is useful if a person generally calls you to tell you he's sending you a fax. (See the next section of this lesson for more information.)

- Choose Don't Answer if you don't want the modem to answer the phone automatically. Note, however, that there is a way to answer if you know a fax is arriving; that is explained in the next section.

5. When you select your option, click OK to return to the Microsoft Fax Properties dialog box. Then click OK again to return to the Exchange mailbox.

Manually Answering the Phone

If you choose Manual or Don't Answer as your configuration option, you can control whether or not the modem answers the phone each time it rings. If you know a fax is arriving, the modem answers; otherwise, it doesn't.

For the Manual answering configuration, when the phone rings, an information dialog box appears, asking if you want to receive a fax (see Figure 12.6).

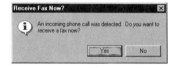

Figure 12.6   The modem knows the phone is ringing and wants to know if you want to answer it.

For the Don't Answer configuration, when the phone rings and you know it's a fax, click the fax machine icon at the right end of the taskbar (next to the clock). The Fax Status dialog box appears (see Figure 12.7), and you can choose Answer Now to force the modem to receive the fax.

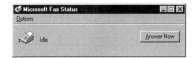

FIGURE 12.7   Open the Fax Status dialog box using the taskbar icon, and then tell the modem to answer the phone.

   Quick Answer   As a shortcut, you can right-click the
TIP   taskbar fax icon and choose Answer Now from the shortcut menu instead of opening the Fax Status dialog box.

VIEWING THE FAX

After the modem answers the phone and receives the fax, the fax is placed in your Inbox. A fax icon appears in the Message Type column so you can tell it's not a regular e-mail message. Often, there's no data available for the From and Subject columns.

Double-click the fax's header to open the Fax Viewer and read the fax message. (If you receive a fax from another Microsoft Exchange Client user, you can treat it as a regular e-mail message, and the usual message window opens instead of the Fax Viewer.)

Faxes that are sent from freestanding fax machines can sometimes be difficult to read. Senders often put the fax in upside down, or it goes through the machine at an extremely crooked angle. Instead of standing on your head or tilting way over, use the tools on the Fax Viewer to rotate the fax as needed. You also can zoom in when the font is too small to read. The tools on the Fax Viewer are easy to use and are self-explanatory (but click Help if you need it).

In this lesson, you learned how you can compose, send, receive, and read faxes from a Windows 95 Microsoft Exchange Client system. In the next lesson, you'll learn how to create and use personal folders.

LESSON 13

USING PERSONAL FOLDERS

In this lesson, you learn how to create, configure, and use personal folders to store messages and files.

Personal folders are useful for storing files and messages you want to keep for your own use. You can collect information from many sources and store it in one place or in multiple personal folders according to a category sorting scheme that works for you.

Personal folders are usually stored on your own hard drive, but you can store them on the server (although doing so reduces the privacy of the folders).

 Server Storage Space Normally, the amount of space that you can use on a server is limited. If you store large amounts of information on the server in personal folders and begin experiencing problems when running programs that access the server, you may need to check if you've used your storage limit on the server.

The capability to have personal folders is not automatic. This feature must be added to your Microsoft Exchange Client profile. If this feature has already been established, there is a Personal Folders object in the Folder pane of your Exchange window. If that object doesn't exist, you will have to add the feature to your profile (see your system administrator if you need help). This lesson assumes you have the capability to add personal folders to your system.

CREATING A PERSONAL FOLDER

The Personal Folder object that appears in your Viewer is the container into which you place all the personal folders you create. There is a plus sign (+) next to the object, indicating that this container has subfolders. By default, there is a Deleted Items personal folder, which provides the same function as the Deleted Items folder in your mailbox: It holds deleted items until you either retrieve them or delete them permanently. (See Lesson 11 for information about the mailbox's Deleted Items folder.)

If a personal folder does not appear in your Folder pane, you can create one by following these steps:

1. Select Tools, Services to display the Services dialog box.

2. From the Available Information Services list, select Personal Folders. Then click OK.

3. Type the name you want for the personal folder file in the File Name box. Make sure that it has a .pst extension.

4. Select the file location from the Look In box, and then click Open.

5. Click OK to close the Personal Folders dialog box.

6. Click OK again to close the Services dialog box.

You can create as many personal subfolders under the Personal Folders folder as you need by following these steps:

1. Select (highlight) the personal folder object, and then choose File, New Folder. The New Folder dialog box appears, as shown in Figure 13.1.

2. In the New Folder dialog box, enter a name for the folder and click OK.

FIGURE 13.1   The name for a personal folder should indicate the items it will hold.

TIP   **Nested Personal Folders**   You can create personal subfolders under any personal folder if you want to maintain files and messages in a sorting scheme that requires it. Just select the parent folder, and then create the new folder while the parent folder is highlighted.

USING PERSONAL FOLDERS

After you create a personal folder, it's easy to place items into it. For example, you can add items to a personal folder in any of these ways:

- Put received messages or attachments into a personal folder by highlighting the item and choosing Copy or Move, and then choosing the personal folder as the target.

- Add files to a personal folder by opening Explorer while the Microsoft Exchange Client Viewer is open and dragging the file from its original directory to the folder. (This system works in Windows 95 and Windows NT 4.0.)

- Copy or move items from one personal folder to another.

- If you have the necessary rights and permissions, copy items from a public folder into a personal folder. (See Lesson 14 for information about public folders.)

To view or manipulate any item in a personal folder, just select that personal folder in the Folder pane, and the items stored in the folder are displayed in the Contents pane. In the Contents pane, double-click the item of interest to open it.

MANAGING PERSONAL FOLDERS

You can create as many personal folders as you need. Some reasons for having multiple folders are to have a separate folder to store messages that you are only copied on or to have a separate folder for archive messages. Every new personal folder you create is, by default, named Personal Folder. If you create multiple folders, you'll need to rename these folders with descriptive names. For example, you may want to name a folder that is set to receive copied messages only "CC's" and the one for saving messages "Archives."

You can make the following decisions regarding the configuration and management functions of your personal folders:

- You can change the name of a personal folder in Microsoft Exchange Client (which also changes the name of the personal folder object in your Viewer).

- You can password-protect your personal folders (which is useful if you store them on the server or if other people share the use of your computer).

- You can compact your personal folders file (get rid of blank spaces as a result of deletions) to save disk space.

To exercise these options, follow these steps:

1. Choose Tools, Services to display the Services dialog box.

2. Select Personal Folders, and then choose Properties. The Personal Folders dialog box appears (see Figure 13.2).

3. Using the options shown here, change the name, add a comment, add or change your password, or compact the folder file. (The following sections provide more information about setting passwords and compacting personal folders.)

4. Click OK to complete the configuration process.

Figure 13.2   You can configure the properties of your personal folders services in the Personal Folders dialog box.

The two most important choices in the dialog box are the password feature and the compacting utility.

The capability to add comments to your personal folder configuration isn't important to the way the personal folder feature works. But you may think of some note you want to write yourself about your personal folders, and you can use the Comment text box to do so.

Password Protection

When you password-protect your personal folders, you are not applying a password to any specific personal folder, you are applying a password to the file that holds all your personal folders. To add a password to your personal folders, follow these steps:

1. From the Personal Folders dialog box, choose Change Password to display the Change Password dialog box (see Figure 13.3).

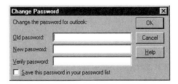

Figure 13.3   When you enter text in this dialog box, you won't see it. It's a secret, so you'll see only stars (****).

2. In the Old Password text box, enter the existing password (if there is one). If there is not one, press Tab to move to the next field.

3. Type the new password, and then press Tab to move to the next field.

4. Retype the new password in the Verify Password box. If the characters don't match the new password, you'll be able to re-enter both the new password and the verify entry.

5. Select Save This Password in Your Password List, if you don't want to type the password each time you use your personal folders.

6. Click OK when you are finished.

 TIP   **Save Password**   If you choose Save This Password, your new password is stored in a password list, and you won't be asked to enter it when you access your personal folders file. However, if someone with a different name is logged on to your computer, or if another user attempts to access your personal folder file from a different computer on the network, the password will be requested.

COMPACTING THE PERSONAL FOLDER FILE

Every time you add a new personal folder or place a message or file into a personal folder, the file that holds the personal folders gets bigger. However, when you delete an item or move an item to somewhere else on your system, the file doesn't shrink itself even though there's less in it. Therefore, as you add more and more items and continue to delete items, the file only gets larger because of the additions and the empty space left by the deleted files.

You can compact the personal folder file to get rid of the blank spots and reduce it to the size needed to hold only the current contents. Of course, as you add new items, it grows again, and it continues to leave behind blank spots when you delete items. So you'll have to compact it from time to time.

To compact the personal folder file, click Compact Now in the Personal Folders dialog box. An informational dialog box appears, informing you that the process is underway and giving you a chance to Cancel if you want to (see Figure 13.4). Compacting can take a few seconds or a few minutes, depending on how many items you have in personal folders.

FIGURE 13.4   Compact your personal folders file to save disk space.

In this lesson, you learned how to create and manage personal folders. In the next lesson, you'll learn about public folders, what they are, and how you can use them.

Using Public Folders

In this lesson, you learn about public folders: what they are and how to use them.

Public folders are used to store items (files, company forms, or any other information) that can be accessed by all the users on your Microsoft Exchange Server system. Public folders are created at workstations by users, but they are stored on the server. (Personal folders, covered in Lesson 13, are kept on the user's local hard drive.)

Understanding Public Folders

Public folders make it easy to distribute information to everyone in the organization. You can place an item in a folder instead of sending it through e-mail to a long list of users. It's a simple way to let everyone read an interesting text file about some topic important to the company's well-being, to distribute the latest company employee handbook, to circulate general announcements about company policies or company events, or to distribute items to those employees who are working together on a project.

Each server in your Microsoft Exchange Server system holds the public folders that have been created by the users attached to that server. Then, at regular periods during each day, the public folders and their contents are replicated to all the other servers in the organization. This way, every user can have access to every folder, regardless of the folder's origination point.

When you see the display of public folders in your Microsoft Exchange Client window, you can't tell the difference between public folders that were created on the server on your site and public folders that were created at other remote servers and replicated onto your own server. But it doesn't matter, because the replication function ensures that there is a copy of every public folder on the server to which you're attached.

By default, no user of Microsoft Exchange Client is permitted to create a public folder. An administrator must either make specific configuration changes to Microsoft Exchange Server to permit the creation of public folders at certain workstations, or create the public folders at the administrator's own workstation. This lesson assumes that someone has been given the necessary rights to create them and that there are some public folders in your system. (If you've been given creation rights, see Lesson 15 for administration information.)

When you look at the display in the Folder pane of your Microsoft Exchange Client window, the top level of public folders is a container folder named Public Folders (see Figure 14.1). Under that folder is a subfolder named All Public Folders, which contains all the public folders for the system. There may also be a Favorites folder displayed. (Information about the Favorites folder is found in Lesson 16.)

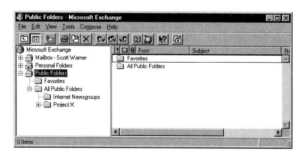

Figure 14.1   The public folders are displayed in a hierarchy that starts with a Public Folder container.

   Container Folder   A folder that is designed specifically to hold other folders. The icon for a container folder differs from that of a regular folder: It depicts a folder sitting in a box.

CHECKING ACCESS PERMISSIONS TO PUBLIC FOLDERS

To open a public folder and view its contents, you must have the necessary permissions for reading a public folder. Likewise, you must have the necessary permissions if you want to add items to a public folder. Company-wide folders are usually created with these rights for every user. Project folders or folders created for specific uses normally give rights to a user list that is associated with the project.

 Permissions   In Microsoft Exchange Server, the administrator sets permissions to spell out the tasks you are permitted to perform, such as reading and writing permissions. Roles have been established that are specific combinations of permissions.

UNDERSTANDING ROLES

Roles are combinations of rights. Various combinations of rights have been put together and assigned a name by Microsoft Exchange Server (and are in turn assigned to users by a public folder administrator). These are the predefined roles and their attendant rights:

- Owners have all permissions.

- Publishing Editors can create, read, edit, and delete items and create subfolders.

- Editors can create, read, edit, and delete items.

- Publishing Authors can create and read items; edit and delete the items they create; and create subfolders.

- Authors can create and read items, and edit and delete the items they create.

- Reviewers can read items.

- Contributors can create items.

To see if you have permission to access a public folder, right-click the folder and choose Properties from the shortcut menu to display the folder's Properties dialog box and select the Summary tab (see Figure 14.2).

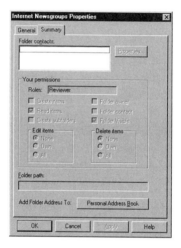

FIGURE 14.2   A Properties dialog box for a public folder.

Your role and the permissions attached to that role are displayed in the Properties dialog box of each public folder. The dialog box also displays the name of the public folder's owner. You can contact that person to get additional permissions.

VIEWING AND WORKING WITH PUBLIC FOLDER CONTENTS

To view the items in a public folder, select that folder in the Folder pane to display its contents in the Contents pane (see Figure 14.3).

To manipulate any of the items in a public folder, right-click the item to bring up the shortcut menu (shown in Figure 14.4).

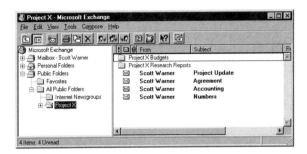

FIGURE 14.3   All the items contained in the public folder are displayed in the Contents pane.

FIGURE 14.4   The shortcut menu lists all the operations you can perform on an item.

> **TIP**   **Quick Open**   The shortcut menu's choice of Open is the default action. So if you want to open an item, just double-click it instead of right-clicking and choosing Open.

Working with public folder items isn't much different from working with messages or files from software applications. Table 14.1 lists the commands on the shortcut menu, along with a description of each.

TABLE 14.1   SHORTCUT MENU OPTIONS

COMMAND	FUNCTION
Open	Launches the software that was used to prepare the item, which in turn displays the item in its window. If the item is a standard message, the message is displayed in the Exchange message window.
Mark As Read	Identifies the selected files, messages, or other items in the folder as having been read or opened.
Save As	Saves the item in a different location. (The Save As dialog box appears, so you can choose a location, a file name, and a file type.)
Move	Moves the item out of the current folder and into a different folder in your Microsoft Exchange Client system.
Copy	Copies the item to another folder in your Microsoft Exchange Client system.
Print	Prints the item.
Reply to Sender	For a message, opens a message window so you can send a reply to the sender.
Reply to All	Opens a copy of the message that is pre-addressed to the sender and all recipients of the original message. You can than write your response to the message either within or above the original message.
Post Reply in This Folder	Enables you to respond to a message that requires a specific *form*.
Forward	For a message, sends a copy to another user.
Delete	Deletes the item (if you have the correct permissions).
Properties	Displays the properties of the item.

Form   A document created and used in Microsoft Exchange Server for a specific purpose. Forms are attached to specific public folders and are used to limit the way items are placed in a public folder. An example of a form is a vacation schedule, an expense report, or any other document that requires you to fill out a preconfigured form instead of entering data.

ADDING ITEMS TO PUBLIC FOLDERS

If you have permission to post to a public folder, you can add an item either by copying the item from another folder in your Microsoft Exchange Client system, or by copying a file created in a software application.

To add a file from your computer file system to an Exchange folder, open Explorer while the Microsoft Exchange Client viewer is open. Then drag the file from its original directory to the folder. (This system works for both Windows 95 and Windows NT 4.0.)

The method in which public folders are implemented, the permissions given to users, and the forms created for individual public folders are all a reflection of the policies and philosophies of your organization. No two companies implement this feature the same way. Your access to public folders will match the manner in which public folders are adapted at your company.

In this lesson, you learned about public folders, how to access them, and how to manipulate their contents. The next lesson teaches you how to administer public folders that you have created.

15 ADMINISTERING PUBLIC FOLDERS

In this lesson, you learn how to perform some of the available administrative tasks on a public folder you've created.

If the system administrator has given you permission to create public folders, any folder you create has your name on it as the owner. The owner has all rights and permissions to a public folder, can establish permissions for other users, and controls the way the contents are displayed in the folder.

SETTING PUBLIC FOLDER PERMISSIONS

As the owner of a public folder, you get to decide which users have rights to access the folder, as well as the extent of those rights.

To configure permissions for a public folder you own, right-click the folder and choose Properties from the shortcut menu. In the Properties dialog box, click the Permissions tab. Figure 15.1 shows the Properties dialog box (with the Permissions tab in the foreground), as it appears to the owner.

By default, all users can access public folders with the role of Author (which has permission to read and create items, see the information posted to the folder, and post her own items to the folder). However, you can change the default role, and you can add users and give them specific rights.

To add users and assign rights, follow these steps:

1. On the Permissions tab, choose Add to display the Global Address List. Then double-click the user you want to add and click OK.

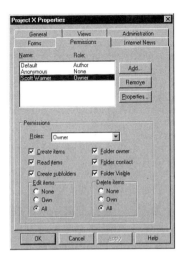

FIGURE 15.1 Use the options on the Permissions tab to give rights for this folder to other users.

2. When the user's name appears on the Permissions tab, the default role is selected. To change the role, click the name to highlight it, click the Roles drop-down arrow, and select a role for this user (see Figure 15.2).

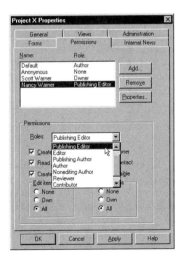

FIGURE 15.2 Choose a role for the user for whom you are currently assigning permissions.

TIP **Change the Default Role** If you want to change the default role for users, highlight that entry and pick another role. If you want to keep out all users except those you specifically designate, you can choose a default role of None.

UNDERSTANDING ROLES

As you've learned, a *role* is a predefined set of rights. When you choose a role for a user, you're actually choosing a specific list of rights. After selecting the rights (they're displayed with a check mark), you can select additional rights or deselect any rights. If the changes you make match the rights assigned to another role, the name of that role appears. If the changes you make create a set of rights that don't match any existing role, the name of the role that appears will be "custom." Refer to Lesson 14 for more information on roles.

CHANGING THE FOLDER'S VIEW

The *view* is the way the information in a folder is displayed when users open the folder. It is a specific organization method of columns, categories, and sort order. You can change any of those items to have some control over what is displayed and the order in which it's displayed.

To configure a view for a public folder, follow these steps:

1. Right-click the desired public folder.

2. Select Properties from the shortcut menu.

3. Click the View tab of the folder's Properties dialog box to see the options shown in Figure 15.3.

4. Choose New to create a new set of criteria for viewing the contents of the folder. The New View dialog box appears (see Figure 15.4), in which you can set up the conditions for displaying the folder's contents.

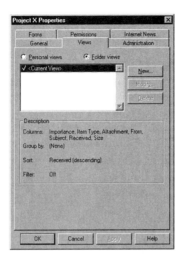

FIGURE 15.3   All the details about a highlighted view are displayed.

FIGURE 15.4   Use the New View dialog box to design the criteria that controls what users see when they open this folder.

5. Enter a name for this view in the View Name box.

TIP **Naming Views** Give each view a name that describes its function. If the view emphasizes the date of messages, name it "By Date." If it emphasizes the sender, name it "By Sender," and so on.

6. (Optional) Choose Columns to display the Columns dialog box (see Figure 15.5). The list on the right shows the columns that will appear in the view. Add columns by selecting them in the Available Columns list and clicking Add. To remove columns, select them from the list on the right and click Remove. In the list on the right, you can move items up or down (which means left or right on the actual folder display) to control the order in which they're displayed. Click OK to return to the New View dialog box.

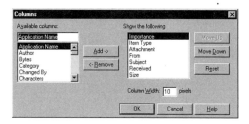

Figure 15.5 Highlight a column name to add or remove it.

7. (Optional) Choose Group By if you want to organize the display of the folders contents into related groups. The Group By dialog box appears, in which you can group contents according to the column categories you've selected. Within each group you can sort (ascending or descending) by any column category. Click OK to return to the New View dialog box.

8. (Optional) Choose Sort to sort the contents by one of the selected column categories. (Use Sort only if you didn't use Group; grouped contents are already sorted.) Click OK to return to the New View dialog box.

9. (Optional) Choose Filter to establish a set of rules that will include or exclude the display of items in this folder (see Figure 15.6). Click OK to return to the New View dialog box.

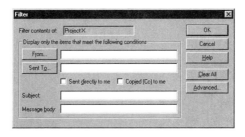

FIGURE 15.6 You can set conditions that items have to match to be displayed in the folder.

10. Click OK in the New View dialog box when you finish setting up the criteria for the new view. Then click OK to close the folder's Properties dialog box.

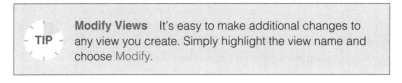

Modify Views It's easy to make additional changes to any view you create. Simply highlight the view name and choose Modify.

TIP

In this lesson, you learned how to impose some rules and control over a public folder you've created. In the next lesson, you'll learn about the Favorites folder, which simplifies your access of public folders.

16 WORKING WITH THE FAVORITES FOLDER

In this lesson, you learn how to use a special folder called a Favorites folder.

UNDERSTANDING THE FAVORITES FOLDER

As the various divisions, departments, and individuals in your organization create public folders for different uses, the list of public folders grows quite long. After a while, it takes time and effort to scroll through all the public folders to find the one you need. And often, many of the public folders are of little interest to you either because you don't have a reason to use their contents or you don't have permission to access them. But unfortunately, you still have to scroll through them.

Instead of crawling through all those public folders, you can use a special folder that stores shortcuts to the public folders you need to access regularly. This special folder is called the *Favorites* folder. The Favorites folder is one of the folders placed under the Public Folders container during the installation of Microsoft Exchange Client. (The other is a container named All Public Folders, below which all the public folders for your company are displayed.)

Shortcut   A shortcut is a reference to (or a pointer to) another object in Microsoft Exchange Server. If you place a shortcut to a folder into your Favorites folder, the shortcut provides a link to its connected folder. The folder itself is not placed in the Favorites folder (that would make it a subfolder). But double-clicking the shortcut actually opens the folder.

ADDING FOLDERS TO THE FAVORITES FOLDER

After you know which public folders you need to access on a regular basis, you can add them to your Favorites folder. Just select the public folder, and then choose File, Add to Favorites or click the Add to Favorites button.

Either way, the Add to Favorites dialog box appears (see Figure 16.1). This dialog box displays the public folder's name and then provides a place where you can enter a new name for this folder that will identify it in the Favorites folder. By default, the original public folder name is used. Click the Add button to accept the default name, or enter a new name in the Favorite Folder Name text box and then click Add.

FIGURE 16.1   Each shortcut to a public folder should have a name that you will recognize.

Favorites by Another Name The original name of a folder is used by default when you add a shortcut for it to your Favorites folder. However, you can use any name that you would like for the shortcut, and it will still point to the chosen folder (even though they will have different names).

ADDING SUBFOLDERS TO YOUR FAVORITES FOLDER

Although a public folder may have subfolders, these subfolders are not automatically added to the Favorites folder when their parent folder is added. To display the choices for adding a folder's subfolders to the Favorites folder, open the Add to Favorites dialog box and click the Options button. The dialog box expands to show the Subfolders section, shown in Figure 16.2.

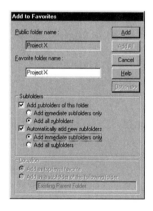

FIGURE 16.2   You must specify if and how subfolders should be added to the Favorites folder.

If you choose to add subfolders, you must also specify to add all subfolders or immediate subfolders only. Click the appropriate option button to indicate your preference. In addition, you can choose to automatically add any new subfolders that are created. This option is a little more complicated, and it depends on the choice you made for the first option:

 Immediate Subfolder A folder that is one level below (subordinate to) any chosen folder. In other words, it is one immediate level below a folder in the folder hierarchy.

- If you chose to add immediate subfolders only and you turn on the option to automatically add subfolders as they're created, Exchange automatically uses the same setting for this option (Add immediate subfolders only).

- If you choose to add all subfolders and you turn on the option to automatically add subfolders as they're created, this choice is independent of the method used to originally add a folder's subfolders to the Favorites folder. Therefore, you can choose whether to automatically add only immediate subfolders as they're created or to add all subfolders as they're created.

USING THE FAVORITES FOLDER

When you want to check the public folders that are important to you, open your Favorites folder, which displays the list of all the public folders you have added to your Favorites list (see Figure 16.3).

Notice that one of the folders, Project X in Figure 16.3, is listed in bold type. This means that the link between the shortcut in the Favorites folder and the original public folder has sent a message indicating there are new items in the public folder. To see the items in the public folder, highlight the item in the Folder pane. The contents appear in the Contents pane, and unread items are listed in bold type.

When you look at the listing in the Contents pane, you are looking at the items in the original public folder, just as if you had scrolled through the public folders to find the real one. The folder listing in the Favorites folder is merely a pointer. It is not really a folder, so it has no contents.

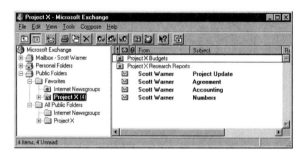

Figure 16.3   The Favorites folder lists your selected public folders.

Removing Folders from the Favorites Folder

There are going to be occasions when your access to a public folder is taken away (perhaps your participation in a project is finished) or when you find that you really have no interest in a public folder that's in your Favorites folder. You can delete a public folder from your Favorites folder by selecting it and pressing Delete. A dialog box appears, asking you to confirm the deletion. Click Yes to proceed, or click No to cancel the command to delete the folder. When you delete a public folder from your Favorites folder, you are only deleting the link (or pointer). The real public folder is not deleted.

 Deleting Favorites   You cannot delete the Favorites folder itself; it is a system folder.

In this lesson, you learned about the Favorites folder. In the next lesson, you'll learn about scheduling your time with Microsoft Exchange Client and Schedule+.

SCHEDULING YOUR TIME WITH SCHEDULE+

In this lesson, you learn how to use the Schedule+ features in Microsoft Exchange Client to schedule your time and keep track of appointments.

Microsoft Schedule+ is a powerful software application capable of performing many tasks. It must be specifically installed on your computer as part of the installation of Microsoft Exchange Client. This lesson assumes that the Schedule+ software is installed and teaches you how to keep your schedule of appointments in Schedule+.

GETTING TO SCHEDULE+

If you are viewing the Microsoft Exchange Client window and want to move to Schedule+, you'll find that you can't get there from here. There is no option for Schedule+ on any of the menu lists. Instead, you have to gain access to the Schedule+ toolbar button. The following steps show you how:

1. Open the Tools menu, choose Customize, and select Toolbar to display the Customize Toolbar dialog box (see Figure 17.1).

2. Scroll through the Available Buttons list box and click Show Schedule to highlight it. (The Schedule+ toolbar button is called Show Schedule.)

3. Click Add to move this button to the Toolbar Buttons list box.

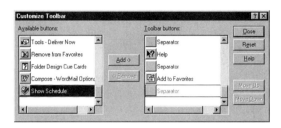

FIGURE 17.1   Use the Customize Toolbar dialog box to put the Schedule+ button on the toolbar.

   Use the Shortcut   Instead of performing steps 2 and 3, **TIP**   you can double-click the button in the Available Buttons list to add it to the Toolbar Buttons list.

4. (Optional) In the Toolbar Buttons list box, click the Show Schedule button and then choose Move Up or Move Down to position it where you want it on the toolbar. (The dialog box says up and down, but the toolbar stretches left to right. So think of Up as Left.)

5. Click Close when you finish. The Show Schedule button now appears on the toolbar. Click it to open Schedule+.

STARTING SCHEDULE+ FOR THE FIRST TIME

To use the features in Schedule+, you have to have a schedule file. So the first time you use Schedule+, you'll be asked to create a schedule file because one doesn't exist. Follow the on-screen directions to complete the process. After that, you can click the Show Schedule button anytime to start the software.

THE SCHEDULE+ WINDOW

When you open Schedule+ for the first time, you might think the program window seems a bit busy and complicated (see Figure 17.2). However, it's really just a logical arrangement of *views*, which are different ways to look at the same information. By default, the window appears in Daily view. To change to another view, click the appropriate tab.

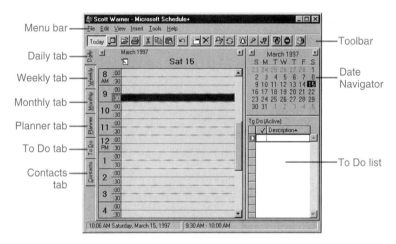

FIGURE 17.2   The Daily view of the Schedule+ window.

Two of the elements of the window shown in Figure 17.2 are unique to the Daily tab: the Date Navigator and the To Do list. These elements are not universal, so they do not appear in all the available views. (You'll learn more about managing tasks and the To Do list in Lesson 19.)

ENTERING AN APPOINTMENT

To keep track of your time, and plan your work, you have to enter your appointments in Schedule+. To learn how to enter appointments, follow these steps:

1. Make sure you're in the Daily view (if you're looking at a different view, click the Daily tab).

2. In the Date Navigator, move to the appropriate month (if the appointment is not in the current month). Then click the day for the appointment. The Daily tab changes to display that date.

TIP **Moving Through the Date Navigator Calendar** The Date Navigator has two arrows, one in each of the upper corners. Click the right arrow to move ahead one month at a time. Click the left arrow to move back one month at a time. You can also use the Alt key in combination with the arrow keys to change the date in the Date Navigator.

3. Click the time slot for your appointment to highlight that line (or drag over multiple time slots).

4. Enter text that describes the appointment.

5. Click anywhere outside the appointment listing to end the entry process. After the appointment is entered (see Figure 17.3), you will see a notation about it on all of the time tabs: Daily, Weekly and Monthly. (The bell icon on the appointment line indicates that you will get a reminder.)

The bell means there will be a reminder.

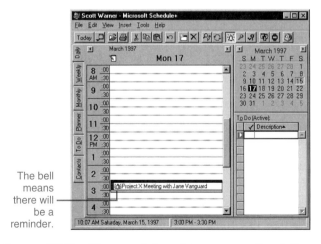

FIGURE 17.3 The appointment appears on the daily calendar.

By default, when you enter an appointment, a reminder is attached to it (the bell icon on the appointment line indicates the presence of the reminder). That means you will see a note reminding you of the appointment ahead of time. You can set the reminder interval (how long before the appointment you want the reminder).

If you don't want a reminder, you can click the appointment line and then click the Reminder button on the toolbar. This button toggles the feature: click on, click off.

You can also enter an appointment by clicking the New Appointment button on the toolbar (see Table 17.1 for more information about the toolbar buttons). If you use this method, an Appointment dialog box appears (see Figure 17.4).

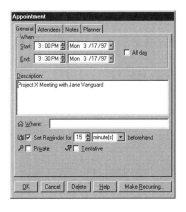

FIGURE 17.4   The Appointment dialog box lets you set options for appointments.

In fact, when you enter an appointment directly onto the Daily schedule, as described earlier, there is actually an Appointment dialog box created in the background. You can see it (and make changes) by double-clicking the left edge of the appointment listing.

VIEWING YOUR SCHEDULE FROM THE OTHER TABS

Click the Weekly tab to see the appointments you've entered displayed in a Monday through Friday pattern (see Figure 17.5). You can select an appointment and manipulate it with the toolbar buttons, or you can edit it by double-clicking it and making changes in the Appointment dialog box. Changes you make are reflected everywhere this appointment appears (in every view).

FIGURE 17.5   The appointment you entered on the Daily tab also appears on the Weekly tab.

If you click the Monthly tab, any appointments you've entered appear on the appropriate date as shown in Figure 17.6. The notation is brief, but you can double-click the entry to display the Appointment dialog box so you can see the details. You can also make changes to the appointment, and those changes will be reflected everywhere the appointment is listed.

The Planner tab also shows your appointment (see Figure 17.7). This tab is intended to help you track your busy times and free times, so details about the appointment aren't displayed. The Planner also has a Date Navigator and an Attendees box so you can set up a meeting for a time that's convenient to all the attendees. See Lesson 18 for more information about setting up meetings with other users.

FIGURE 17.6   The Monthly tab displays appointments in a calendar form.

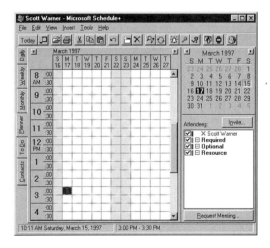

FIGURE 17.7   In the Planner tab, the block of time your appointment fills is marked to indicate you're busy at that time.

ADDING OPTIONS TO YOUR APPOINTMENT LISTING

There are a number of special features and options you can apply to an appointment after you enter it. Some of them are available through the toolbar. Table 17.1 lists the toolbar buttons and their functions.

TABLE 17.1   TOOLBAR BUTTONS FOR SCHEDULE+

BUTTON	NAME	FUNCTION
Today	Today	Moves the schedule to today
	Go To Date	Opens a small Date Navigator calendar
	Open	Opens another schedule file
	Print	Prints the schedule's data
	Cut	Moves selected text to the Clipboard
	Copy	Copies selected text to the Clipboard
	Paste	Pastes the Clipboard's contents
	Undo	Undoes the last action
	Insert New	Opens a dialog box for a new entry; the entry changes to match the tab you're on (appointment, task, contract)

BUTTON	NAME	FUNCTION
	Delete	Deletes the selected item
	Edit	Displays the Appointment dialog box so you can make changes
	Recurring	Makes the appointment a recurring one (daily, weekly, monthly, and so on)
	Reminder	Sets the reminder feature for this appointment
	Private	Hides the appointment from other users
	Tentative	Places the item in your schedule, but not in the schedule viewed by other users
	Meeting Wizard	Launches the Meeting Wizard, which walks you through the process of scheduling meetings with other users
	Timex Watch Wizard	Transmits data to a special Timex Watch you can purchase
	View Mail	Switches to the Microsoft Exchange Client window

There are other options for appointments available in the Options dialog box. Open the Tools menu and choose Options to see the choices (see Figure 17.8). These are global options, meaning they are the default for every appointment you enter. Take some time to look them over, and also look at the options available on the Defaults tab. You may want to change your default settings if the current options don't suit you.

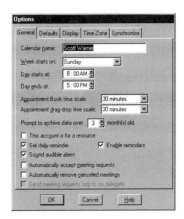

FIGURE 17.8   Set options about reminders, warnings, and other scheduling features with the Options dialog box.

SYNCHRONIZING YOUR SCHEDULE

A copy of your appointment schedule is kept on the server so that other users of Microsoft Exchange Server can learn when you're free or busy in order to schedule meetings. Exchange Server regularly checks your schedule to keep the network up to date on your plans.

In this lesson, you learned how to open the Schedule+ software, enter an appointment, add options to appointment listings, and make a copy of your schedule available to other users. In the next lesson, you'll learn how to use Schedule+ to set up meetings.

Setting Up Meetings with Schedule+

In this lesson, you learn how to use the Schedule+ software to schedule meetings with other people in your organization.

Scheduling a meeting involves quite a few steps:

- You have to decide who should be there
- You have to find out when those people are available
- You have to select a meeting time that's convenient for all attendees
- You have to decide on a place for the meeting
- You have to notify all the attendees of the meeting's time and place
- You have to track the responses so you know how many (and which) attendees will be at your meeting

Whew! That's a lot of work. You won't have time to get much else done. Luckily, there are two features available in Microsoft Exchange Client that can make all of this faster and easier: the Microsoft Exchange Server Free/Busy folder and the Microsoft Exchange Client Meeting Wizard.

Free/Busy Microsoft Exchange Server has a container stored on the server called the Schedule+ Free/Busy folder. All users attached to that server have their Schedule+ meetings synchronized to this folder. The folder is replicated to other servers in the organization (and those servers also replicate their Free/Busy folders) so that it's possible to learn the free and busy times in every user's schedule.

USING THE MEETING WIZARD

The Meeting Wizard is a Microsoft Exchange Client feature that walks you through all the steps it takes to set up a meeting with other users. To use the Meeting Wizard, follow these steps:

1. Click the Meeting Wizard button on the toolbar. The meeting wizard opens, as shown in Figure 18.1.

FIGURE 18.1 Specify the type of attendees and resources you'll need for this meeting.

2. In the first dialog box (see Figure 18.1), select the options you need for this meeting. Then choose Next.

3. In the next dialog box, click Pick Attendees to see a list of all users. Select the required attendees and choose Next.

4. If you specified a need for optional attendees, enter those names on this page. Then choose Next.

5. To enter the location you want to use for your meeting, choose Pick Locations and select a location from the Global Address List (double-click the location to select it and click OK). Choose Next.

6. (Optional) You can enter more than one location and let the Wizard determine which to use (based on availability). Choose Next.

7. (Optional) If you chose the option to schedule resources (such as computers or A/V equipment) in the opening Wizard dialog box (refer to Figure 18.1), you will also have to select those resources here. The resource dialog box follows the location dialog box.

TIP   **Locations and Resources**   It's important that companies create users and mailboxes for shared locations and resources. These facilities are used for meeting arrangements, and schedules must be kept for them. Locations are also for sending e-mail. For example, the research library or the audio-visual room might want to send mail to users about new equipment, or users might want to send mail to a location requesting information about facilities. If your organization maintains conference rooms, equipment, or similar facilities and they're not listed in the Global Address List, ask your administrator to remedy that.

8. Enter the expected duration of the meeting and the travel time to the meeting. Then choose Next.

9. Enter the acceptable times and days for this meeting (see Figure 18.2). This information will be matched against the free and busy times of the attendees. Choose Next.

10. (Optional) If there were optional attendees specified for this meeting (refer to Figure 18.1), the Wizard asks if their free/busy schedules should be checked. If you're listing them because you merely want them to know that the

meeting is taking place, answer No. If you want them
to attend (if they're free), answer Yes. This affects the
Wizard's determination of a good meeting time.

FIGURE 18.2   Specify a range for the start and end times and
select the acceptable days for your meeting.

Entering Non-Existent Names   If you enter a location or
a resource that isn't listed in an address list, you can use
the Check Names button. This button is used to check
typed entries against existing entries. If your entry isn't
listed, you are given the opportunity to add it to the
address list. If you add the location or the resource to
the address list but don't use the Check Names button,
you'll have to do it later. The Wizard won't complete the
scheduling process and issue the invitations with any
information that can't be confirmed against the users
and locations known to your Microsoft Exchange Server
system.

TIP   **Travel Time**   The travel time is important. If you are
holding the meeting outside of the office, give the attendees an indication of how long it will take to get to the
meeting place so that when attendees' schedules are
checked, the travel time can be factored into the decision
about each person's availability.

Now that you've entered all the information, the Wizard takes over. The entities involved in your meeting plan (attendees, locations, and resources) are checked for free and busy times. If any entity has not been diligent about keeping a schedule, the Wizard will report that fact. Figure 18.3 shows a report on a problem location, and Figure 18.4 reports a problem with an attendee. Click OK on any of these informational dialog boxes.

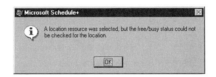

FIGURE 18.3   The people in charge of the conference room haven't made a schedule, so the server's free/busy folder has no information.

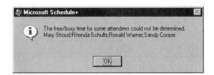

FIGURE 18.4   Users who don't keep schedules make it difficult to schedule meetings.

USING THE WIZARD'S RESULTS

When all the Free/Busy schedules have been checked, the Meeting Wizard displays the information it has gathered (see Figure 18.5).

Most of the time, unless all the attendees you selected are incredibly busy people, the Meeting Wizard offers you a choice of meeting times. The original Wizard report displays the next available time at which all the criteria you set for attendees and resources are met.

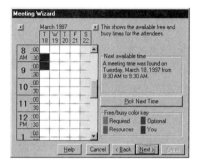

Figure 18.5   The Meeting Wizard shows free and busy times and suggests a meeting time.

You can look at another possible meeting time by choosing Pick Next Time. Additional meeting dates are then displayed, in chronological order. If you want to go back to the original meeting date, click the left arrow at the top of the calendar that displays the free/busy times. The next available time that's displayed will back up to match the calendar section you click on.

 Do It Yourself   In case you don't like any of the times the Wizard picked, you can view the free/busy information for all the attendees and resources. There's a color code key on the dialog box, so you can decide which attendee or which resource you want to give up to have the meeting on a date that doesn't match all the schedules. To schedule this meeting, however, you'll have to issue the invitation messages manually.

When you have selected one of the Wizard's proposed dates, choose Next. The last Meeting Wizard dialog box appears, announcing that the Wizard has done its job and telling you that the next step is to issue the invitations to all attendees. Choose Finish.

SENDING THE INVITATIONS

The Meeting Request form automatically appears when the Meeting Wizard finishes (see Figure 18.6). All the information necessary to notify the attendees is already filled in (optional attendees are in the Cc box). If you want to, you can add a note to the text. When you're satisfied with the information, click the Send button to send the meeting notice. The meeting is then added to your schedule.

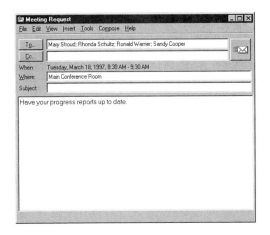

FIGURE 18.6   All the necessary information is already filled in when the Meeting Request form appears.

In this lesson, you learned how to use the Meeting Wizard to set up a meeting based on the attendees' free and busy times. In the next lesson, you'll learn how to manage tasks using Schedule+.

19 MANAGING TASKS WITH SCHEDULE+

In this lesson, you learn how to use the Schedule+ software to track tasks and projects. You learn how to enter tasks into your To Do list and how to connect tasks with specific projects.

A *task* is an item in a list of things to do. It can be related to a project, or it can be an independent chore that you're responsible for. Tasks also can be recurring. For example you may have to turn in an expense report every month, or you may have to send out invoices every week.

ADDING TASKS TO YOUR TO DO LIST

To track a task, you need to tell your Microsoft Exchange Client system about it. There are actually two ways to add a task: the quick and easy way (which inserts the task into your To Do list) and the less quick but more detailed way (which lets you set a priority, end date, and other information about the task).

ADDING TASKS THE QUICK WAY

The fast way to insert a task into your To Do list is to use the Daily tab, which is in the foreground by default when you first launch Schedule+. Follow these steps to use the quick method of adding a task:

1. Click the To Do section of the Daily tab.

2. Click the first available row, and it becomes highlighted.

3. Type a name or description of the task (see Figure 19.1).

4. Press Enter, and the task appears as a regular entry in your To Do list.

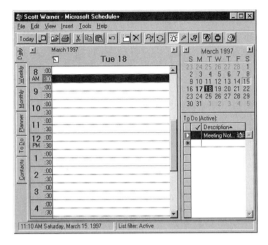

FIGURE 19.1 You can enter a task in the To Do list of the Daily tab.

When you enter a task in this quick way, certain defaults are assumed about the task's characteristics. Based on those assumptions, the task is assigned to the current date (the date displayed in the Daily tab), it has a priority of 3 (see the discussion on priority later in this lesson), and its duration is set for one day.

ADDING TASKS WITH DETAILS ATTACHED

If the task is a bit more complicated and needs to be configured for a date range, with a priority, or using other details, you can provide this information by using the Task dialog box to set up the task. Just follow these steps to create your task:

1. Click the To Do tab. The full To Do window appears (see Figure 19.2).

2. Click the Insert New Task button to display the Task dialog box shown in Figure 19.3.

3. If the task will take more than a day, click the Ends check box and specify the date on which the task will end. (You can click the down arrow next to the entry box to see a Date Navigator, from which you can select a date.)

Figure 19.2 The To Do tab displays the tasks you're tracking, along with information about them.

Figure 19.3 The Task dialog box lets you configure a task with many options.

4. In the Starts box, specify the number of days, weeks, or months *before the end date* that the task starts. (Click the down arrow to choose whether you're specifying days, weeks, or months.) This is the task's start date.

5. Click the Mark As Done After End Date check box if this task definitely ends on the specified end date.

6. In the Description box, type a brief description of the task.

7. In the Project box, enter the name of the project to which this task is linked (if there is one). You can enter a new project, or you can click the drop-down arrow and choose an existing project from the list that appears.

8. In the Priority box, set the level of importance for this task. (Use the up and down arrows to scroll through the priority choices.)

TIP

Task Priority Levels   As you scroll through the available priority choices, you'll see the numbers 1 through 9 and the letters A through Z. The numbers appear on the right side of the Priority box, and the letters appear on the left. You can take advantage of this by creating all sorts of priority schemes, including choosing a letter and then a number to end up with a priority such as C3. It's a good idea to work with other people in your company to establish some pre-determined meanings for the available priority indications.

---

9. (Optional) Check the Set Reminder box to enable the reminder feature. When you select this option, two additional selection boxes appear, in which you can specify the number of minutes, hours, days, weeks, or months before the start date (or the end date) that you want to see a reminder.

10. (Optional) Check the Private box if you don't want this task to be seen by other users on the network.

11. (Optional) Click the Make Recurring button if this task fits that category.

12. When you finish setting the details, click OK. The task is now listed on your To Do list.

Marking a Task As Complete

When you finish a task, you will want to mark it off the list. There's a quick way to tell Schedule+ that you've completed it. Click the box to the left of the task description on the Daily tab to indicate you've completed this chore (see Figure 19.4). That column to the left of the description is the "check off" column: You check off the task when you're done. A check mark appears in this box when you click it to show that the task has been completed.

Click here when
you've completed
the task.

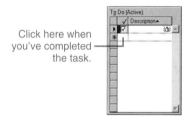

Figure 19.4 Check off the task when it's been completed.

Managing Projects

A *project* is a goal-oriented group of tasks. For example, you can have tasks such as "collect budgets from department heads," "import General Ledger into database," and other related tasks as part of the project called "Budget Review for 3rd Quarter." After you've created your project, you can link your tasks to it by using the Project option in the Task dialog box (refer to Figure 19.3), as described in the previous section.

There are two methods for adding a Project to your To Do list:

- Enter a project name into the Project box of the Task dialog box, as described in the previous section. This adds the project and gives it a default priority of 3.

- Choose Insert, Project and use the Project dialog box to give the project a name and a priority. Figure 19.5 shows the Project dialog box.

FIGURE 19.5 Use the Project dialog box to give the project a title and a priority.

Project names appear in bold on the To Do list, and their priority levels are indicated in parentheses. You can click the plus button next to the project name to see the list of tasks linked to the project.

There are a couple of things you should know about the relationship between projects and their linked tasks:

- The priority for a project is not automatically inherited by its tasks; each of the tasks can have whatever priority you choose.

- If you make the project private, all of the tasks linked to the project are also made private.

In this lesson, you learned how to add tasks to your To Do list, and you learned about projects and how to link tasks to projects. In the next lesson, you'll learn how to use Schedule+ to manage information about the people you must contact.

20

MANAGING CONTACTS WITH SCHEDULE+

In this lesson, you learn how to use the Schedule+ software to track and manage all the people you contact for business or for personal reasons. You also learn how to use the information you accumulate in a productive way.

The jargon for this type of software is "contact management," and it's more than just a little black book. You can use your contact listings to quickly enter appointments or tasks related to specific contacts, or you can group contacts that share a common bond so you know who has to be contacted when a particular issue arises.

ENTERING CONTACTS

To enter information about a contact, move to the Contact tab and click the Insert New Contact button on the toolbar. This brings up the Contact dialog box (see Figure 20.1), which has four tabs. The Business tab is selected by default when you open the dialog box. To move to a different tab, simply click it.

Use the Business tab to enter information about this contact. Its fields are self-explanatory (refer to Figure 20.1). Use the Phone tab, shown in Figure 20.2, to track all the phone numbers for this contact.

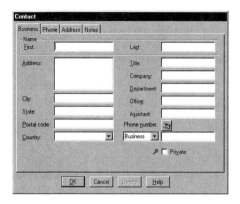

FIGURE 20.1   The Business tab of the Contact dialog box lets you enter information about this contact.

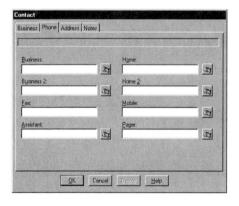

FIGURE 20.2   You can track every type of telephone number for a contact.

When you look at either the Business tab or the Phone tab, you see icons that look like a telephone. If you have a telephone attached to your modem, you can click one of the telephone icons, and your modem will dial the number next to the icon. Your modem line becomes a voice line, and you will be prompted to lift the receiver to talk to the person you called. Of course, you have to have a telephone instrument attached to your modem to take advantage of this feature. After you call a contact once, the contact's name is placed in a *calling log* that functions as part of your contact tracking efforts (see Figure 20.3).

FIGURE 20.3 If you have a modem you can call this contact with a click of the mouse.

Calling Log When you click a telephone icon to make a call to a contact, it is added to a log. The log's file name is CALLLOG.TXT, and it's located in the directory where your Windows operating system is installed. This is a plain text file that you can open with any text editor (or any of the text word processors that came with your operating system). There is a line of text for each call you made to a contact, including the name, telephone number, date, time, and duration of the call. You should make sure to edit this file occasionally so it doesn't grow too large to work with comfortably.

The Address tab provides a place to store a home address and phone number for the contact, in addition to the spouse's name, the contact's birthday, and the date of the couple's anniversary.

The Notes tab is a place for you to write comments or notes to yourself about this contact. In addition, this tab provides four user-definable fields, named User 1 through User 4, that you can use to enter data that helps you sort your contact list. For example, you might decide to use the User 1 field to indicate your relationship with this contact. You can invent codes so that the data you enter in User 1 is consistent, such as Family, Customer, Vender, and so on. Then you can select contacts by code to produce a list you can use for a specific purpose.

After you finish filling out the information in the Contact dialog box, click OK. The name is added to the list on the Contact tab (see Figure 20.4).

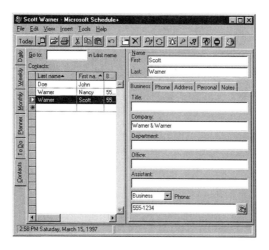

FIGURE 20.4   Click a name, and the related details appear on the right side of the window.

The list is on the left side of the window. When you select a contact in the list, details about that contact appear on the right side of the window. You can click any of the tabs to display the information you need.

 TIP   **Quick Contact Entry**   You can also enter information about a new contact right at the Contact tab listing. Just click the first blank row, enter the last name, press Tab, and then enter the first name. You can then enter the detailed information in the appropriate places on the right side of the window.

CONNECTING TASKS WITH CONTACTS

If you need to follow up with a contact, perhaps by making another telephone call or sending information, you can create a task that's connected to the contact. To do so, follow these steps:

1. Click the appropriate contact name to select it.

2. Click the right mouse button to see the shortcut menu.

3. Choose Task from Contact. When the Task dialog box opens, the contact's name is in the Description box (see Figure 20.5).

Figure 20.5   Link a task to a contact using the shortcut menu, and the contact name is automatically inserted in the Description box.

4. Enter additional text to remind you of the task (for example, add the word "call" in front of the contact's name).

5. Set the date for the task and any priority specifications you need, and then click OK.

Connecting Appointments with Contacts

In much the same way you connect a task with a contact, you can use the shortcut menu to connect an appointment with a contact. To try it, follow these steps:

1. Click the contact name to select it. Then right-click it to see the shortcut menu.

2. From the shortcut menu, choose Appt. from Contact. The Appointment dialog box opens with the contact's name in the Description box.

3. Specify the date, time, and place.

4. (Optional) Set a reminder if you want to.

5. Click the Attendees tab to add any additional attendees.

6. Click OK when you finish entering information into the dialog box. The appointment is displayed in your schedule.

7. (Optional) If you have invited additional attendees, a Meeting Request message form appears, with the attendees listed in the To box and all the necessary information already filled in. You can add a note if you want to. Then click the Send button.

SORTING YOUR CONTACTS LIST

You can sort the contacts in your Contacts list by several criteria. To establish a sorting scheme, follow these steps:

1. Choose View, Sort to display the Sort dialog box (see Figure 20.6).

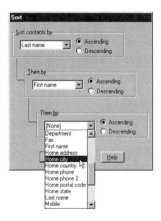

FIGURE 20.6   You can choose any category to sort and sub-sort your contacts list.

2. In the Sort Contacts By list box, select a category for the
   first level sort. Then select categories in the two Then By
   boxes to set up secondary sorts. All the categories from all
   the tabs of the Contact dialog box are available as sort
   options.

3. Specify Ascending or Descending for each sort level.

4. When you finish, click OK. Your Contacts list is sorted
   by the categories you selected. The sorting scheme you
   design becomes the default for your Contacts tab.

 TIP **Only One Sort Level Is Required** You don't have to use
all three sort levels when you design your sorting scheme.
There is a choice of "none" available, and you can select
it for level 3 (or for both level 2 and level 3) if you want to.

 TIP **Quick Sort** Instead of trying to enter new contacts in the
correct sort order in your Contacts list, you can just enter
new names on the blank lines of your Contacts list. Then,
after you've completed all your entries, choose View, Sort
Now. The new entries are placed on the list according to
your default sorting scheme.

In this lesson, you learned how to enter and manage contacts and
how to link those contacts to tasks and appointments. In the next
lesson, you'll learn about delegating mail functions so that others
can take over some of your e-mail chores (or the other way
around).

DELEGATING MAIL FUNCTIONS

In this lesson, you learn how to delegate mailbox functions so that you can arrange to have someone else take care of some or all of your e-mail. In addition, you learn how you can take care of another user's mail.

UNDERSTANDING DELEGATION

In Exchange, *delegation* is the act of permitting someone to represent you. In Microsoft Exchange Client, you can arrange to have a delegate do one or all of the following things:

- **Open your mailbox and view the contents.** You can make arrangements to be notified about those messages that are important and then decide whether the delegate should respond to them.

- **Send mail on your behalf.** Messages sent from your mailbox by the delegate have the delegate's name along with the words "on behalf of" followed by your name in the From field of the message.

- **Send mail in your name.** Messages sent from your mailbox by the delegate have your name as the sender. The receiver has no reason to think the mail is not from you.

To delegate responsibilities, you have to perform two separate operations: You must give the delegate access to your mailbox; then you must specifically configure your mailbox to permit the delegate to send mail on your behalf. If you also want the delegate to send mail in your name, you must have an administrator make configuration changes to your mailbox at the server; you cannot provide that right yourself.

Providing Access to Your Mailbox

To have a delegate access your mailbox (or specific folders in your mailbox) you must configure your mailbox for the necessary permissions. To accomplish this, follow these steps:

1. In the Folder pane of your Microsoft Exchange Client window, select your mailbox. If you are giving permission for a specific folder only, such as the Inbox, select the folder.

2. Right-click the mailbox and choose Properties from the shortcut menu to bring up the Mailbox Properties dialog box.

3. Click the Permissions tab to see the options shown in Figure 21.1.

Figure 21.1   Use the Permissions tab to give specific rights to your mailbox to other users.

4. Click Add to see the Global Address List, and then double-click the delegate's name. (You can name more than one delegate.) Click OK when you finish adding names. The delegate's name appears on the Permissions tab.

5. Select (highlight) the delegate's name. Then click the Roles drop-down arrow, select a role, and click OK.

HANDLING CONFIDENTIAL MAIL

If you're used to having an assistant or secretary open all your mail and you want to extend this duty to e-mail, you can, but note that there's no way to exclude confidential or personal items that you receive at that e-mail address. The only way to get around this is to have the administrator create a second mailbox, a *hidden mailbox*, for you. Then you can give out that address to people who need to send you confidential or personal mail.

TIP   **Hidden Mailbox**   Microsoft Exchange Server enables an administrator to hide a mailbox so that it isn't displayed on any address lists. However, if a sender types in the mailbox name when he's filling out the To section of a message, the message will get to the mailbox. To use this feature, you have to give the hidden mailbox name to anyone who needs to send you confidential mail, and then you must check that mailbox yourself.

ACCESSING ANOTHER USER'S MAILBOX

If you have permission to access another user's mailbox, you have to take these few steps:

1. Choose Tools, Services to display the list of services installed in your profile.

2. Select Microsoft Exchange Server and choose Properties.

3. Click the Advanced tab to move to that page (shown in Figure 21.2).

Figure 21.2   You can add the capability to open additional mailboxes if you've been given the permissions.

4. Choose Add to add another item to the Open These Additional Mailboxes list.

5. Enter the name of the additional mailbox you've been given permission to access.

6. Click OK. Then click OK two more times to close the dialog box. Your folder list now displays the additional mailbox along with your own mailbox (see Figure 21.3).

You can manipulate the new mailbox the same way you handle your own mailbox.

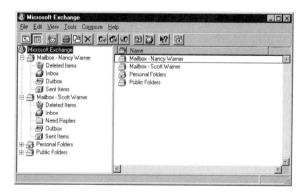

Figure 21.3   The Folder pane shows all the mailboxes to which you have access.

DELEGATING THE SEND MAIL FUNCTION

When you let a delegate send mail on your behalf, the From field of all messages sent by this delegate contains the words "Sent on behalf of" followed by your name, along with the delegate's name.

To authorize a user to send mail on your behalf, follow these steps:

1. Choose Tools, Options.

2. Click the Exchange Server tab of the Options dialog box (see Figure 21.4).

3. Place the delegate's name in the Give Send on Behalf Of Permission To box by choosing Add, selecting a name from the address list that appears, and double-clicking the selected name.

4. (Optional) Repeat step 3 to add additional delegates.

5. When you finish selecting delegates, click OK. Then click OK again to close the dialog box.

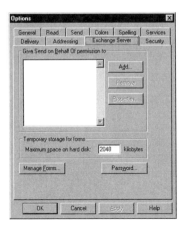

FIGURE 21.4 Choose the delegate that you want to send mail throughout the system on your behalf.

SENDING MAIL AS A DELEGATE

After all the permissions are set, your delegate can begin sending mail on your behalf (or in your name if the administrator has configured this option for you). If you are the delegate, you can send mail on another user's behalf from your own mailbox. It's just like sending a message from yourself to another user, except you have to change the name in the From field. To send mail on another user's behalf, follow these steps:

1. Click the New Message button to open a new message form. By default, this form does not display a From box in the header, so you have to remedy that.

2. Choose View, From Box to insert a From box in the message window.

3. Move your pointer to the From box and either type in the other user's name or click From and select the name from the Global Address list that appears. You do not have to add anything else; Microsoft Exchange Server takes care of adding the information that this message is written on behalf of the other user.

4. Fill in the rest of the message header, placing the recipient's name in the To box, entering additional recipients in the Cc box, and filling in the Subject box.

5. Move to the text box and enter the message.

6. Click the Send button to send the message.

If you do not have the proper permissions to fill in the From box with another user's name, Microsoft Exchange Server will issue an error message and refuse to send the message. Of course, if the administrator has established delegation rights for sending mail in the name of the user, the recipient will not be able to tell that the delegate composed and sent the message. The From box merely gives the user's name.

In this lesson, you learned how to give permissions for others to access your mailbox and how to send mail on behalf of others. In the next lesson, you'll learn how to use the Inbox Assistant to automate some of the tasks you perform when you receive mail.

Using the Inbox Assistant

In this lesson, you learn how to manage incoming mail with automatic procedures, using the Microsoft Exchange Server feature called Inbox Assistant.

What Is the Inbox Assistant?

The Inbox Assistant is a feature that lets you establish automatic procedures that will be performed on all your incoming mail. For example, you might want to set up automatic procedures to perform the following actions:

- Reply to incoming mail under certain conditions that you establish

- File incoming mail in specific folders using criteria you establish

- Forward incoming mail under certain conditions that you establish

You can use the Inbox Assistant to manage your mail, and it works whether or not you have your Microsoft Exchange Client software open. In fact, you don't even have to have your computer on, because the work for the Inbox Assistant is done at the server (where your mailbox is located).

There are two things you have to do to put the Inbox Assistant to work:

- Create a set of conditions (called rules) for the Inbox Assistant to look for when it examines incoming mail

- Create a set of actions for the Inbox Assistant to begin whenever the conditions have been met

CREATING RULES

Creating a rule is a simple process, but you can create an enormous number of permutations and combinations to cover any (and all) possibilities. This example creates a scenario that tells the Inbox Assistant that whenever a message comes from the Payroll department, you want it moved to a specific folder in your mailbox. This would be helpful if you had given an associate permission to that folder, and the associate was to take care of all the timesheets and other payroll issues for you. To work through the example scenario, follow these steps:

1. Choose Tools, Inbox Assistant to display the Inbox Assistant dialog box.

2. Choose Add Rule, which brings up the Edit Rule dialog box (see Figure 22.1).

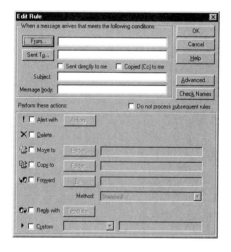

FIGURE 22.1   The Edit Rule dialog box lets you configure the rules and the resulting actions for the Inbox Assistant.

3. In the top part of the dialog box (labeled "When a Message Arrives That Meets the Following Conditions"), specify the conditions that the message has to meet to cause any action to occur. In this case, you want to

specify that the message must be from the Payroll department.

Click From to indicate you want to base this rule on the sender. Then select the appropriate name(s) from the Global Address List by double-clicking the name(s) in the list (you can select as many names as you want). When you finish, click OK.

Narrowing the Rule   You'll have to do some homework for some of these rules to work. For example, in this scenario, you might have one user named Payroll, which is a mailbox shared by all members of the Payroll department; or you might have one member of the Payroll department who is the only person that ever sends e-mail about payroll issues; or you might have to list every person in the Payroll department just to make sure you've covered all the possibilities.

4. Choose an action from the bottom section of the dialog box (labeled "Perform These Actions"). In this case, choose Move To and click Folder. The Move Message To... dialog box appears, as shown in Figure 22.2. From this dialog box, choose the folder you want to move these messages into and click OK.

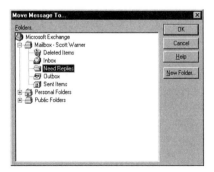

FIGURE 22.2   You can automatically move a message into any folder in your Microsoft Exchange Server system.

Picking a Folder You can choose any folder in your
Microsoft Exchange Server system as the destination for
messages you're moving or copying. If you pick a mailbox
folder or a public folder, Microsoft Exchange Server will
take care of the move for you, even if you're working in
Microsoft Exchange Client at your computer. If you
choose a personal folder (which resides on your local
hard drive), Microsoft Exchange Server will not complete
the Inbox Assistant's work until you launch your software
and are connected to the server. At that point, the message is moved into the specified personal folder.

5. Click OK again to close the Edit Rule dialog box. As you
can see in Figure 22.3, the new rule is listed in the Inbox
Assistant dialog box.

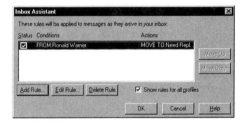

FIGURE 22.3   All the rules you create are listed in the Inbox
Assistant dialog box.

Set Multiple Rules This exercise was a simple one: You
set one rule with one condition. You can, however, set
multiple rules. Perhaps you want a rule that says "if the
message is from Payroll and the subject is Overtime Reports, perform this action." Just continue to set rules until
all your conditions are established.

Turning Off a Rule

If you want to abandon a rule temporarily for some reason (perhaps your assistant is on vacation and you'll have to take care of all your mail yourself), you don't have to delete the rule and then re-create it. The Inbox Assistant dialog box contains a Status box for each rule (refer to Figure 22.3). Click to select or deselect the rule. When a rule is selected it's turned on; when it's not selected, the rule is turned off.

In this lesson, you learned how to set conditions and actions so the Inbox Assistant can handle mail automatically. In the next lesson, you'll learn how to use the Out of Office Assistant to automate the handling of mail when you're not at work.

23 ^{LESSON} USING THE OUT OF OFFICE ASSISTANT

In this lesson, you learn how to use the Out of Office Assistant to manage your incoming mail automatically when you're not in your office.

If you're going to be out of your office, you can use the Out of Office Assistant to deal with incoming mail. For example, you could automatically send a note to each person who sends you mail, saying you're away and giving instructions on who to direct questions to (such as "contact Bob in my absence"). Or, you could forward a copy of all (or certain) messages to a coworker.

As with the Inbox Assistant (which you learned about in Lesson 22), you have to create rules for the Out of Office Assistant to follow.

SENDING OUT OF OFFICE NOTES

The most common function of the Out of Office Assistant is to send a note back to every person who sends you e-mail. The note, which you compose, can inform the sender of your absence, ask the sender to contact someone else, or say whatever else you might want to say. The Out of Office Assistant keeps track of the names of people who send you mail, and it sends only one note to each person.

To have the Out of Office Assistant send a note to everyone who sends you e-mail during your absence, follow these steps:

1. Choose Tools, Out of Office Assistant to bring up the Out of Office Assistant dialog box.

2. Click in the AutoReply... text box and enter the message you want to send to people who send you mail in your absence (see Figure 23.1).

FIGURE 23.1   Enter a message for the Out of Office Assistant to send while you're away from your office.

CREATING AUTOMATIC RULES

You also can create a set of rules for automatic handling of your incoming mail while you're away from your office. The rules can be applied in addition to the AutoReply feature.

FORWARDING MAIL

One common practice that makes use of this feature is to make sure that messages marked high priority are forwarded to another user for instant action. To establish this rule, follow these steps:

1. Choose Tools, Out of Office Assistant to open the Out of Office Assistant dialog box.

2. In the Out of Office Assistant dialog box, click the Add Rule button.

3. When the Edit Rule dialog box appears, choose Advanced.

4. From the Advanced dialog box (see Figure 23.2), select Importance, choose High from the list box of priority choices, and click OK.

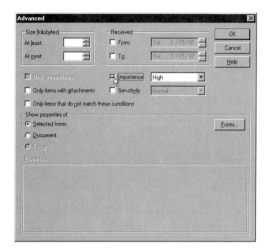

Figure 23.2   You can set specifications for the kind of messages you want handled automatically while you're away.

5. From the Perform These Actions section of the Edit Rule dialog box, choose an action. In this case, choose Forward, click the To button, and select (double-click) the user who will receive this message. Then choose OK. The rule appears in the Out of Office Assistant dialog box (see Figure 23.3).

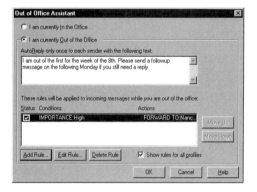

Figure 23.3   The AutoReply features and the rules you've set take effect only when you're out of the office.

6. Click OK to close the Out of Office Assistant dialog box. Neither the rule nor the AutoReply feature will be implemented until you select the I Am Currently Out of the Office option button.

CREATING OTHER RULES

As you saw in the previous exercise, arranging for high-priority messages to be forwarded is a simple process. While you were creating this rule, you may have noticed the other possibilities for creating rules. You can create rules based on certain conditions, such as who sent the message, whom the message was sent to, and whether it contains a certain word. In addition, you can have the message moved, copied, forwarded, deleted, or replied to. With this large range of conditions and actions, rules and the actions they perform can range from a very simple rule that has one condition and performs a single reaction to a rule that has many conditions and performs several reactions.

RETURNING TO WORK

After you return to your office, when you launch your Microsoft Exchange Client software, you'll be reminded that the Out of Office Assistant is enabled (the I Am currently Out of the Office button is selected). Open the Out of Office Assistant (choose Tools, Out of Office Assistant) and select the I Am Currently in the Office option button.

 Conflicting Rules If you've enabled the Inbox Assistant, it's always in effect. If any of the rules you establish in the Out of Office Assistant conflict with the rules in the Inbox Assistant, during the time you are out of the office, the Out of Office Assistant's rules will take precedence.

In this lesson, you learned how to use the Out of Office Assistant to handle incoming mail when you are not in your office. In the next lesson, you'll learn how to access information from a Microsoft Exchange Server using a Web browser.

24 ACCESSING EXCHANGE FROM A WEB BROWSER

In this lesson, you learn how to access the information contained on an Exchange Server using any frames-capable Web browser.

The recent popularity explosion of the World Wide Web has fueled the introduction of many new Web-based applications. These applications make access to information easier and greatly simplify the maintenance of a company's applications. Exchange Server comes with such an application. This application is a group of Web pages that allow users to interact with an Exchange server. It allows you to log on to Exchange Server, check your mailbox, send mail, view and post to public folders, and even set certain options for your mailbox. Even users without a mailbox can use some of these Web pages to interact with Exchange's public folders. In addition to this included application, custom applications can be built to access the information contained on the Exchange Server.

Whether it is the application included with Exchange or a custom solution, such applications allow users to access Exchange servers from remote locations. This is useful for people who travel a lot and don't want to take up space on a laptop with the Exchange client software. As long as they have a Web browser and a way to connect to the network containing the Exchange server, they can interact with the server as if they were sitting at their desks.

LOG ON TO AN EXCHANGE SERVER

To access personal information, follow these steps:

1. First, log on to the server. You must know the Internet address of your Exchange Server to do this. Use your Web browser to move to the correct address (see Figure 24.1).

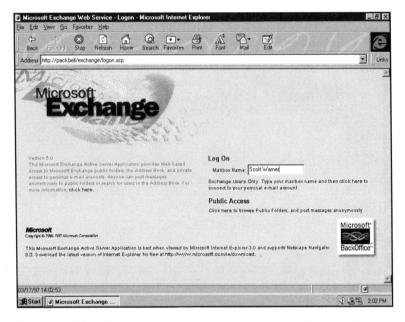

FIGURE 24.1   You can log on and access personal information, or you can just view public folders.

 Know Your Server Address   Your server's address may be a name or a group of numbers separated by periods. It may be on an intranet or located at a remote site that you connect to over the Internet. If you do not know the address of your server, contact your system administrator.

2. Enter your mailbox name and press Enter. Your request to view your mailbox is sent to the server along with your user name and password. If you are successfully logged on to the server, you will see a page that displays the contents of your mailbox (see Figure 24.2).

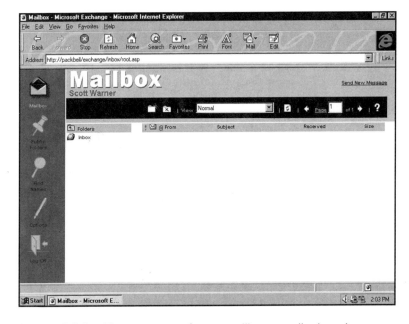

Figure 24.2   The contents of your mailbox are displayed on a Web page.

This Web page supports the most common functions found in the Exchange Client software. From within the mailbox, you can perform any of these actions:

- Create a new folder
- Delete the current folder
- Check for new messages
- Scroll to the previous or next page
- Get help
- Send a new message

Navigating Between Folders You navigate among folders by moving up or down in the folder hierarchy. To move from the Inbox folder to the Sent Items folder, for example, you must first go up one folder.

SENDING A MESSAGE

To send a message, click Send New Message at the top right of the page. This opens the Compose New Message page (see Figure 24.3).

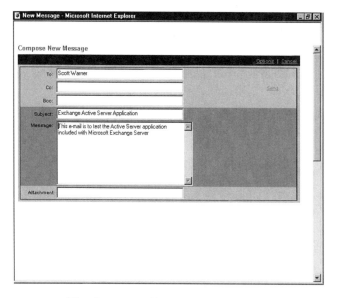

FIGURE 24.3 The Compose New Message page is very similar to the New Message dialog box of the Exchange Client software.

You must enter the recipient information (To:, Cc:, and Bcc:) manually. You cannot access the Global Address List from this page. However, you can still search for display names using the Find Names feature. Enter the subject and message text as usual. If this message has attachments, you must also enter the path and file name manually in the Attachment text box.

You can also set options for a message by clicking the word Options (at the top right of the page) Figure 24.4 shows the Message Options screen that appears. From the Importance drop-down list, choose the importance of the message. Then use the check boxes to indicate whether you want a copy stored in the Sent Items folder and whether you want to be notified when the message is delivered to and/or read by the recipient. When you finish setting these options, click the words Return to Message.

 Sending Attachments Be careful when sending attachments while attached to Exchange using a Web browser. Sensitive data should only be sent over secure connections. And if you are connected over a phone line, be prepared for it to take a long time to send a large file.

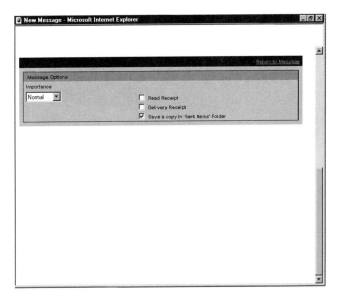

FIGURE 24.4 A message has several optional parameters.

When you are ready to send the message, click the word Send, which is in the right side of the recipients section (of the Compose New Message screen). If you have changed your mind and do not want to send the message, click the word Cancel in the upper-right corner of the page. You will see a confirmation dialog box when the message is sent.

RECEIVING A MESSAGE

Click the Check for New Messages icon to retrieve new messages in your mailbox. Messages are displayed in the Inbox folder according to the view that you have chosen (see Figure 24.5).

The Check for New Messages icon

FIGURE 24.5   The Inbox displays messages you have received.

You can click the underlined name in the From column to read any message. This displays the message in a new Web browser window (see Figure 24.6).

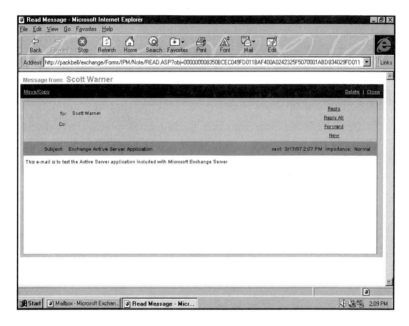

FIGURE 24.6   Each message appears in its own browser window.

The commands available from this page are obvious from the underlined text in the upper-right of the page. Each bit of underlined text performs a different function. From the message window you can perform the following actions:

- Move or copy the message to another folder
- Delete the message
- Close the message
- Reply or forward the message
- Create a new message

PUBLIC FOLDERS

Click the Public Folders icon on the left side of the main Mailbox page to see a list of public folders. The page shown in Figure 24.7 appears. Notice that the Public Folders icon changes when it is the current view.

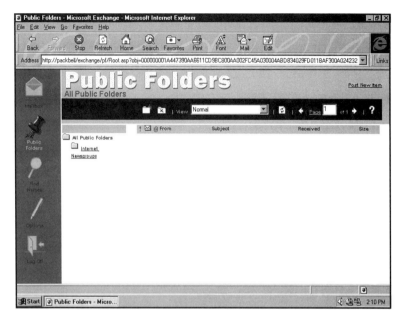

FIGURE 24.7   The Public Folders view.

You can view all public folders and their contents from here by navigating the folder hierarchy. In addition, you can post new items using the Post New Items page.

TIP

Public Folders   You can view public folders and anonymously post to them without logging on to Exchange Server. This feature allows users who do not have a mailbox on the Exchange server to participate in discussions carried out in public folders. To use this feature, click in the Public Access area of the Log On page (refer to Figure 24.1).

FIND NAMES AND OPTIONS

While you cannot open the Global Address List directly from a message page, you can still search for display names using the Find Names feature. Click the Find Names icon to open the Find Names page (shown in Figure 24.8).

FIGURE 24.8   Enter information that you know to find a display name.

After you enter the information that you know or can remember, click the word Find. The search results then appear in the lower portion of the page. Choose one of the display names listed there to get more detailed information on that person.

If you click the Options icon, it opens the Options page (see Figure 24.9). This page allows you to use the Out of Office Assistant. Choose whether Exchange should treat you as in or out of the office. If you choose out of the office, you can supply a default message to be sent to anyone who sends you a message.

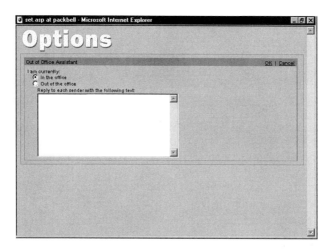

FIGURE 24.9   Use the Out of Office Assistant from anywhere that you have Web access to your Exchange Server.

LOG OFF EXCHANGE SERVER

When you finish working with Exchange Server, you should log off to avoid security problems. Do this by clicking the Log Off icon. You should see a page with some information about logging off. To log off, close the Web browser.

In this lesson, you learned how to access the information on the Exchange Server from a Web browser. In the next lesson, you'll learn how to set up Microsoft Exchange Client software so you can work at a different computer, either at home or on the road.

25

WORKING OFFLINE

In this lesson, you learn how to take all the steps necessary to work from an offsite location.

Working offline is when you're not connected to your network server because you're offsite. When you're not at the office, you have to have some tools available that let you work on a remote computer; then later (when you're back in the office) you have to get the information on your office computer matched up with your offsite computer.

UNDERSTANDING OFFLINE COMPUTING

When you're working in Microsoft Exchange Client at your office, you're connected to a Microsoft Exchange server computer and the two computers interact continuously. When you work at home or when you're traveling, and you can't connect to the server, you do your work *offline*.

When you are offline, you don't have access to the elements of your Exchange system; therefore, the objects that are stored on the server aren't available to you. The server objects are your mailbox (and all its folders) and all the public folders. The only components that are on your local drive are the personal folders you've created.

To take care of this situation, Microsoft Exchange includes a set of tools that let you work on some of these folders on a remote computer, and then either dial in from an offsite location to connect to the server, or connect to the server when you return to the office and synchronize the contents of your folders.

Working offline is different from using Exchange through a Web browser in several ways. The most important is that you do not have to be connected to a network to do your work. This is important for two reasons. First, your company may not allow remote access to their Exchange servers. In this situation, working offline is your only choice when at a remote location without a network connection. Second, it may be inconvenient or too expensive to use the Web access feature. If you are doing your work on an airplane or in another country, it may be too cost prohibitive to use the Web access feature. This may also be true if you have a large amount of work to do. Finally, you may simply prefer the Exchange client interface to the Web interface.

PREPARING TO WORK OFFLINE

You have to set up your Microsoft Exchange Client software to prepare for working offline. This is not difficult and should only take a few minutes.

There are two steps involved in getting ready to work offline:

- You need to prepare the computer you'll be using offline by installing the Microsoft Exchange Client software.

- While you're connected to the network, you need to tell Microsoft Exchange Client that certain folders must be available for offline work.

If you're using a portable computer, you usually can connect to the network (or your office computer for access to the network) through cables. From a home computer or other offsite computer, you'll have to connect via telephone lines. Have the administrator assist you in setting up the hardware and software necessary to use these connections.

PREPARING FOR OFFLINE FOLDERS

An *offline folder* is a replica of a folder that is stored on the server. Mailbox folders and Favorites folders are the folders available for offline work.

You have to tell Microsoft Exchange Client that a folder (or multiple folders) will be used offline. You do this so that the system knows it has to synchronize the offline folder with the folder on your office computer. You only have to do this once.

Synchronize Normally, when you copy a file or folder between computers, the contents of the source file replace the contents of the target file. Synchronization, however, is a process by which Exchange looks at the contents of both folders and then places information in both so the contents are identical. This means you can work offline and also work online, and then you can synchronize your work so that both folders have all the work you've done in both places. (This is not unlike the Briefcase option in Windows 95 and Windows NT 4.0 workstation.)

To make a folder available offline, follow these steps:

1. Right-click the Mailbox folder or the Favorites folder, whichever you want to make available offline.

2. Choose Properties from the shortcut menu, and then click the Synchronization tab of the Properties dialog box (see Figure 25.1).

3. In the This Folder Is Available section, select When Offline or Online. Then click OK.

4. When the information dialog box about the offline folder file appears, click Yes to create the file.

5. In the Offline Folder File Settings dialog box (shown in Figure 25.2), choose an encryption setting or choose no encryption.

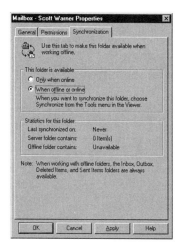

FIGURE 25.1   The online/offline choices and information about synchronization are found in the folder's Properties dialog box.

FIGURE 25.2   You have to establish the configuration for your offline folder file.

Encryption   Exchange can encrypt the file so it cannot be read outside of the Microsoft Exchange Client software. The choice between the two encryption schemes should be made based on whether or not you are using file compression on your hard drive. If you are, choose Compressible Encryption.

6. Accept the default name EXCHANGE.OST for the offline folder file. If the system administrator feels a different file name should be chosen, enter that.

7. When you finish making your choices, click OK. Microsoft Exchange Client creates the file.

DOWNLOADING THE ADDRESS BOOK

To work offline, you should have an address book on your offline computer. Of course, Exchange's Address Book is kept on the server. When you are working offline and can't get to the server, you'll need a copy of the Address Book so that when you click a button to see a list of users, the information is available. You can download the Address Book by following these steps:

1. Open the Tools menu, point to Synchronize, and choose Download Address Book.

2. From the Download Offline Address Book dialog box (shown in Figure 25.3), choose one of the following formats for the Address Book.

   - Choose Download Offline Address Book to move all the data in the Address Book to your hard drive. Select this choice if you want details about users (such as telephone numbers, titles, and so on) or if you are going to be sending encrypted messages.

   - Choose Download Offline Address Book Without Details Information if you only need access to mailbox names.

3. Click OK.

Now when you work offline, the Address Book is available. This means you can run Microsoft Exchange Client, compose messages, place files into folders, and do many of the tasks you do when you're in the office and connected to the network. The difference is that everything is being stored on your offline computer instead of being placed on the server.

FIGURE 25.3 You can choose whether to download all the details in the address book.

COMING BACK ONLINE

When you reconnect to the server and launch Microsoft Exchange Client, the synchronization process makes sure the folders contain identical items. At this point, you can send the mail you composed to all the appropriate user mailboxes. To synchronize your folders, open the Tools menu and choose Synchronize. Then choose This Folder to synchronize only the selected folder or All Folders to synchronize all folders.

In this lesson, you learned how to establish the tools to work offline on a computer that isn't permanently connected to your network.

INDEX

W-X-Y-Z

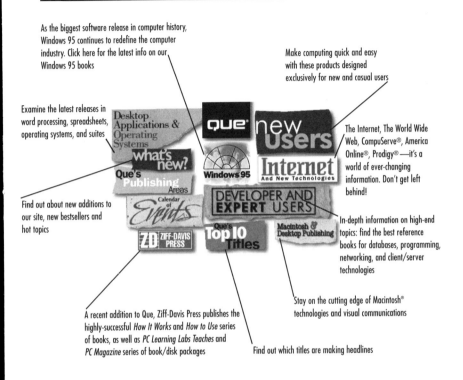

MACMILLAN COMPUTER PUBLISHING USA
A VIACOM COMPANY

Technical ----- Support:

If you need assistance with the information in this book or with a CD/Disk accompanying the book, please access the Knowledge Base on our Web site at **http://www.superlibrary.com/general/support**. Our most Frequently Asked Questions are answered there. If you do not find the answer to your questions on our Web site, you may contact Macmillan Technical Support **(317) 581-3833** or e-mail us at **support@mcp.com**.

Complete and Return this Card
for a *FREE* Computer Book Catalog

Thank you for purchasing this book! You have purchased a
superior computer book written expressly for your needs. To
continue to provide the kind of up-to-date, pertinent coverage
you've come to expect from us, we need to hear from you.
Please take a minute to complete and return this self-addressed,
postage-paid form. In return, we'll send you a free catalog of all
our computer books on topics ranging from word processing to
programming and the internet.

Mr. ☐   Mrs. ☐   Ms. ☐   Dr. ☐

Name (first) ☐☐☐☐☐☐☐☐ (M.I.) ☐ (last) ☐☐☐☐☐☐☐☐☐☐☐☐

Address ☐☐☐☐☐☐☐☐☐☐☐☐☐☐☐☐☐☐☐☐☐☐☐☐
        ☐☐☐☐☐☐☐☐☐☐☐☐☐☐☐☐☐☐☐☐☐☐☐☐

City ☐☐☐☐☐☐☐☐☐☐ State ☐☐ Zip ☐☐☐☐☐☐☐☐

Phone ☐☐☐ ☐☐☐ ☐☐☐☐ Fax ☐☐☐ ☐☐☐ ☐☐☐☐

Company Name ☐☐☐☐☐☐☐☐☐☐☐☐☐☐☐☐☐☐☐☐☐☐

E-mail address ☐☐☐☐☐☐☐☐☐☐☐☐☐☐☐☐☐☐☐☐☐☐

1. Please check at least (3) influencing factors for purchasing this book.

Front or back cover information on book .... ☐
Special approach to the content .... ☐
Completeness of content .... ☐
Author's reputation .... ☐
Publisher's reputation .... ☐
Book cover design or layout .... ☐
Index or table of contents of book .... ☐
Price of book .... ☐
Special effects, graphics, illustrations .... ☐
Other (Please specify): _____ ☐

2. How did you first learn about this book?

Internet Site .... ☐
Saw in Macmillan Computer
    Publishing catalog .... ☐
Recommended by store personnel .... ☐
Saw the book on bookshelf at store .... ☐
Recommended by a friend .... ☐
Received advertisement in the mail .... ☐
Saw an advertisement in: _____ ☐
Read book review in: _____ ☐
Other (Please specify): _____ ☐

3. How many computer books have you purchased in the last six months?

This book only .... ☐   3 to 5 books .... ☐
2 books .... ☐   More than 5 .... ☐

4. Where did you purchase this book?

Bookstore .... ☐
Computer Store .... ☐
Consumer Electronics Store .... ☐
Department Store .... ☐
Office Club .... ☐
Warehouse Club .... ☐
Mail Order .... ☐
Direct from Publisher .... ☐
Internet site .... ☐
Other (Please specify): .... ☐

5. How long have you been using a computer?

Less than 6 months .. ☐   6 months to a year ..... ☐
1 to 3 years .... ☐   More than 3 years ...... ☐

6. What is your level of experience with personal computers and with the subject of this book?

	With PC's	With subject of book
New	☐	☐
Casual	☐	☐
Accomplished	☐	☐
Expert	☐	☐

Source Code — ISBN: 0-7897-1310-1

7. Which of the following best describes your job title?

Administrative Assistant .... ☐
Coordinator .... ☐
Manager/Supervisor .... ☐
Director .... ☐
Vice President .... ☐
President/CEO/COO .... ☐
Lawyer/Doctor/Medical Professional .... ☐
Teacher/Educator/Trainer .... ☐
Engineer/Technician .... ☐
Consultant .... ☐
Not employed/Student/Retired .... ☐
Other (Please specify): .... ☐

8. Which of the following best describes the area of the company your job title falls under?

Accounting .... ☐
Engineering .... ☐
Manufacturing .... ☐
Marketing .... ☐
Operations .... ☐
Sales .... ☐
Other (Please specify): .... ☐

9. What is your age?

Under 20 .... ☐
21-29 .... ☐
30-39 .... ☐
40-49 .... ☐
50-59 .... ☐
60-over .... ☐

10. Are you:

Male .... ☐
Female .... ☐

11. Which computer publications do you read regularly? (Please list)

_____
_____
_____
_____
_____
_____
_____
_____
_____
_____

Comments: _____
_____
_____

Fold here and scotch-tape to ma

NO POSTAGE
NECESSARY
IF MAILED
IN THE
UNITED STATES

BUSINESS REPLY MAIL
FIRST-CLASS MAIL PERMIT NO. 9918 INDIANAPOLIS IN

POSTAGE WILL BE PAID BY THE ADDRESSEE

ATTN MARKETING
MACMILLAN COMPUTER PUBLISHING
MACMILLAN PUBLISHING USA
201 W 103RD ST
INDIANAPOLIS IN 46290-9042